ASPECTS OF
ASHFORD

D.M. & J.L. Barker

INTRODUCTION

This collection of photographic images of Ashford, Middlesex, is another contribution to the ever growing corpus of publications devoted to what was once a small village in rural Middlesex. We have been delighted to research the captions, which we hope will introduce some new aspects of the local history to residents past and present. My own interest in the heritage of the area was formed more than fifty years ago, encouraged by teachers and others to whom local history was important, and it has been a particular pleasure to renew this connection and draw together via the medium of the photograph some of the themes which make the area so interesting.

The work has been made possible by the unstinting help and cooperation of a number of individuals and organisations. In particular we wish to thank Barry Dix, whose title "Ashford Past and Present" is now sadly out of print and Graham Smeed, whose wholehearted cooperation has made the work possible. The collections of Spelthorne Museum (now based at Staines Library) and the S.A. Oliver Trust were also invaluable sources. The active help and cooperation of the Friends of the Museum and its Honorary Curator, Mr. Ralph Parsons, were vital. We also gratefully acknowledge the help of numerous current and past residents who have contributed to the work with memories or loans of original material. One of the aspects of the area on which we are pleased to focus is Ashford's place in the forefront of postcard publishing, with the work of William Henry Applebee, originally highlighted by Graham Smeed, given suitable prominence. We have also endeavoured where possible to note the publisher or photographer of other views included.

We hope that the range and diversity of the material gathered here reflects some of the themes specific to Ashford, for example the remarkable range of educational establishments and the phenomenal growth of the area from the late 19th century, together with some illustration of the more unusual "Aspects of Ashford."

DAVID BARKER
November 2006

FRONT COVER
a) The badge of Abbotsford School, introduced 1958 based on the arms of Middlesex County Council, the town Tree and the River Ash.
b) A selection of the range of local postcards published by John William Smyth c. 1905.

Dedicated to the photographers of Ashford, past, present, and future.

ALEXANDRA ROAD c. 1920

Over the gable of the corrugated iron roof in the foreground can be seen the inscription "Primitive Methodist Church". The denomination broke away from the main body of Methodism in 1807 and was reported as being particularly successful in evangelising agricultural and industrial communities at open-air meetings. Ashford Common's congregation originally met in Laurel Cottage, Napier Road, the first recorded service being on 9th April, 1888. By October 1893, however, the church had moved to this building in Alexandra Road. Along with the local housing, the church at this time had no mains services, gas and water arriving in the 1920s, electricity in 1930. In 1932 the Primitive Methodists, Wesleyan Methodists and United Methodists came together to form the Methodist Church of Great Britain. The following year the premises were extended with new facilities including a schoolroom. This accommodation was soon in use by the wider community with the introduction of a Maternity and Child Welfare Centre by the County Council in 1929. The present church on the site opened in 1960.

THE POST OFFICE, ASHFORD COMMON, c. 1910

Allan Treadaway's grocery store had existed in its prominent position on the corner of Alexandra Road and Staines Road West since c. 1890. Around 1895 it expanded its operation and incorporated a sub-post office and in 1928 the Parish Council were asking the postal authorities for a phone kiosk and stamp machine here, and in 1930 for a pillar box. This facility lasted for more than a hundred years until October 1997 when the post office moved a short distance to 249 Staines Road West. The adjacent premises of butcher's John Adams and its accompanying slaughterhouse can be seen illustrated on page 60 of "Memories Are Made of This". Alexandra Road is said to have been named after the wife of King Edward VII – a Danish princess who married the then Prince of Wales on 10th March, 1863. The area of Ashford Common was the last to receive a number of services: lack of mains gas meant that the street lighting proposed in 1910 was based on oil lamps on standards produced by the Chertsey firm of Herrings.

POST OFFICE, ASHFORD COMMON, c. 1905

The provision of Post Office services in the commercial world is nothing new – in fact the majority of sub-post offices established in the 19th century were, as now, run as an adjunct to various retail enterprises. Ashford Common's facility was part of a large general store. This photograph also illustrates the fact that multi-national companies are not a recent phenomenon. The special display of Puritan Soap was promoting a product of The Granite Soap Company of Newburgh, Maine, USA, founded in 1885. Also seen are some of the other accoutrements of the contemporary home laundry scene: tin- or zinc-coated washtubs, kettles for heating water and soapboxes, useful for both children and politicians. Wealthier residents of the immediate and wider area also had at the time the services of a number of local commercial laundries offering a weekly collection and delivery service. For the majority of Ashford Common's housewives, however, relatively soft water drawn from wells, boiling, scrubbing and mangling followed by starching and ironing was probably the normal routine.

ASHFORD COMMON MISSION ROOM, NAPIER ROAD, c. 1920

During the curacy of the Rev. Alfred Thornton, a mission was established at Ashford Common to cater for the spiritual and temporal needs of upwards of 1,000 residents, including the adjacent district of Cambridge Road, Littleton. This area, at that time lacking many of the services available to other local residents, was also the focus of activity by the Primitive Methodists. The church itself was originally sited in Staines Road and described as an "ancient Church of England mission room". The 1906 trust deed of the new place of worship prohibited its use for "any sort of Council, National or Public Elementary School at any time and to be used for Church of England sponsored bodies only." Support for the mission seems to have waned after the First World War, with fewer regular services being held here. Following the 1930 Local Government reorganisation, which saw Ashford Common amalgamated with Sunbury Urban District Council, St. Benedict's ceased to be part of Ashford Parish and was finally transferred to the charge of the Vicar of St. Saviour's on 1st May, 1940.

STAINES ROAD WEST CROSSROADS, 1907 & 1920

"The Hamlet of Ashford Common is composed of an inn, a smithy and a few cottages which cluster about the crossroads from Staines, Kingston, Littleton and Feltham. Here again building operations are in progress and a few hundred yards to the west there are already several streets laid out on which workmen's houses are being built." This brief description is a contemporary view of the area as published by the Victoria County History of Middlesex in 1911. The history of the area, however, is just as complex and interesting as that of the rest of Ashford. The two views illustrate some of the area around the crossroads and perhaps show that the written record should be treated with caution. Ignored by the V.C.H., the Black Dog, advertising good beds and stabling, should surely qualify as an Inn – a licensed premises offering accommodation – rather than the contemporary listing as a beer house. The importance of the old turnpike route, although it is not fully made up for vehicular or pedestrian traffic, is also illustrated by the routing of telegraph poles. Although the road in the 1920 view is still unmacadamized, sharp eyes will spot the increased capacity of the telephone and telegraph lines in the intervening years. Locals and travellers alike had a choice of hostelries and of Staines or Isleworth brewed beers. The now vanished "Spelthorne" at one time advertised that it was the only licensed premises of its name in the country. At this time the landlord was Thomas William Kent, who had an important sideline. Licensee from 1907 to 1933, he was also a contractor for cartage for the Middlesex County Council, Sunbury and Staines District Council, this strategic position at the crossroads no doubt aiding the enterprise.

ROWLAND'S c. 1930

Elijah Rowland's distinctive premises at Staines Road West was a feature of the area for some 70 years. Mr. Rowland came to Ashford Common in 1923 to build a bungalow, after serving 22 years in the Royal Artillery. His ironmongery business started when he was approached by a number of people for help with acquiring sundry building material for their own projects. From a small store with a flat above, a large enterprise evolved. Within ten years the company had expanded to contain 13 separate departments catering for all manner of building materials: timber, ironmongery, etc. Other sections retailed fuel and motor accessories, cutlery, clocks and patent medicines! Some of this stock can be seen here; later views illustrate the distinctive gallery which ran the length of the façade. By 1933 a branch had been established at 21 Feltham Road and a "Shop on Wheels" retailed paraffin and other necessities. Besides managing the business, Mr. Rowland was also heavily involved in numerous local charities in the Sunbury and Ashford areas, including church and scouting bodies. The shop was sold in 1987 and leased to Brown's Building Supplies. It closed in 1997.

ASHFORD MANOR c. 1930

Richard Ellis, "Royal Servant", was, it is now believed, one of Henry VIII's falconers, recorded as receiving payment from the Sovereign of 41s. 4d. in 1540 and 1541. The site of his dwelling, leased to him in 1542, was strategically situated for serving his royal master, being equidistant from Oatlands and Hampton Court and also convenient for Henry's other local establishments at Kempton Park, Hanworth, Windsor, Byfleet, Woking and Chobham. The grant of the lease to this important Royal retainer was on similar terms to those given to others of Henry's Court who came to dwell in his favourite hunting areas: for example, estates at Sayes Court, Addlestone and Ashley Park, Walton-on-Thames were also leased at 21s. p.a. One of Ellis' charges would probably have been a gyrfalcon, the largest of all hawks and reserved for the use of the Monarch, although whether these birds, with their 5-ft. wingspan, were housed or trained at Ashford is not known. It is, however, satisfying to record that where now Eagles, Albatrosses and Birdies are sought, Tudor Ashford may well have been home to a "Mews " for the royal raptors.

5

ASHFORD MANOR GOLF CLUB, 1928

Some indication of the old field boundaries can still be seen after three decades of the layout of the golf course and alterations to the greens and bunkers. By the late 18th century, taxation records provide evidence of licensed gamekeepers here and the estate seems to have been maintained partly with shooting in mind. The sale of the manorial lands in 1848 advised prospective purchasers that, apart from the designated farmland, the remainder consisted wholly of plantations affording cover for game. Phil Pulley's detailed 1998 history of Ashford Manor Golf Club, "A Hundred Years", also makes reference to a number of features on the course named "zarebas" which may have been the remains of "hides" constructed to afford cover for the guns. Another indication of a vanished way of life can be inferred from a 1904 description of the adjacent Kingston Road as Rabbit Warren Road, a reminder of the days when the animals were artificially confined to provide food or possibly, as here, as quarry for hawks.

KINGSTON ROAD c. 1910

The anomalous horse-drawn coach and four passing through late Edwardian Ashford was not lost in a time warp but part of a short-lived revival of coaching due mainly to the enthusiasm of Alfred Gwyne Vanderbilt and others. From 1908 to 1914 he ran a series of coaches mainly on the route from London to Brighton, including the "Venture" and the "Meteor". Another possibility is a run to Ascot Races, as the "new" coaches were known to have called there and passed through Staines. Experiments were made along the Kingston Road in 1904 with methods of alleviating the ever-growing problems of dust clouds thrown up by the new motor traffic. This included laying tarmacadam, described as the road material of the future, the visit of a deputation from the Automobile Dust Commission and the siting of a new street watering post on the road. However, the photographic evidence clearly shows that fast horse-drawn traffic on the gravelled turnpike route would equally have caused problems for earlier travellers through Ashford!

ASH / FORD BRIDGE c. 1914

The demolition and reconstruction of the bridge over the Ash in 1921 seems to have encouraged discussion in the Parish Council about the provision of swimming facilities for the youth of Ashford. A swimming place was proposed by the Ford Bridge, as the river ran through the site and would keep the place clean. A pool 50 ft. x 25 ft. with changing facilities would cost £1,500 and provide work for the local unemployed, the local labour bureau reporting that 100 Ashford men were out of work in December 1921. Ashford had a Juvenile Swimming Club at the time, but no place for swimming! After some investigation it was decided that the river was too small and shallow; and it was to be another 15 years before the open-air pool adjacent to the Ash at Fernlands was opened. However, pressure from local councillors continued and in 1930 the new Staines Urban District Council's surveyor was instructed to draw up plans and estimate the cost for a bathing place here.

FORD BRIDGE c. 1922

As well as providing the etymological evidence for early occupation, the Ash served a strategic purpose for all the early occupants, acting as a natural boundary and water source, and was no doubt also utilised as a source of food in the form of wildfowl, fish, eels and herbs. The value of the ford here, pre-dating the earlier bridge, is clear – as well as human passage, valuable stock could be watered without risking steep or slippery banks. By the late 13th century the river also seems to have powered a watermill – almost certainly undershot. The origin of the name "Ashford" relates either to an immigrant's personal name or to an older, possibly prehistoric, name for water. Indeed pre-English and pre-Roman names for rivers and watercourses are well represented in the area – the Thames, Wey and Bourne being examples. Long-suspected and recently confirmed archaeological evidence of prehistoric occupation in the west of the parish adjacent to the course of the river suggests to this author that the origins of the place name are ancient and that almost everywhere in Ashford was suitable for early occupation.

FORD FARM c. 1914

Its location commemorated by the eponymous Ford Close and Farm Road, Ford Farm had many connections with aspects of Ashford's history. The farm as seen here also illustrates the adjacent water meadow, a feature of the local topography which no doubt contributed to its long use as a dairy farm, together with the lush, well-watered herbage so valuable to over-wintered cattle. A wide range of buildings associated with the farm is in evidence including barns, cart-sheds and a single-storey structure which by analogy was probably a granary. The farm seems to have been tenanted by a number of dairy farmers in occupation for short periods. The advertisement of C.W. Cuming & Sons, resident here in 1934, gives an indication of the area served, with "Milk delivered twice daily in Ashford, Staines, Bedfont, Laleham, Sunbury and Feltham. All milk bottled on the farm. We supply fresh farm milk or Pasteurised milk." By 1937 builder Herbert Wallage was using the farm as a depot and in July 1938 Middlesex County Council had approved the acquisition of the property for future road widening.

SWIMMING POOL, FERNDALE ROAD, 1936

Captured by Kingston Road photographer W.J. Fair, the opening ceremony in May 1936 of Ashford's new leisure facility was an event of great interest for the area. The continuing pressure from local councillors and others for a local swimming pool (see P. 7) coincided in the mid-1930s with a national drive to improve the health of the nation by the provision of playing fields and other facilities. Many open-air "Lido" type pools were opened at this time. Ashford's Ferndale pool being a typical example of the type erected by local authorities. Taken from the viewing area, the photograph shows that the weather on the day was cold enough to encourage the wearing of overcoats by spectators. Local Councillor Charles Adamson, aged 79, who took the first plunge, described the conditions as arctic! In the pool, giving displays, were children from the nearby Residential School, who had had their own heated indoor pool since 1919. The new facility was an instant success and was also much in use by local schools during the summer term for swimming galas. At the deep end of the pool, adjacent to the Ash, can be seen the diving boards, later supplemented by a platform for more adventurous entry into the 7 ft. of water. The new facility soon had another use when, in September 1939, part of the concrete building was sandbagged for use as an Air Raid Precautions Post. The changing cubicles were curtained and by January 1958 Staines Urban District Council still declined to provide doors for these: they were however in place by c. 1960.

WEST DISTRICT SCHOOL c. 1925 and 1946

Although more than half a century has elapsed since its closure, the West London District School was a major feature of Ashford's recent past. The sheer scale of the institution is apparent here: the extent of the main three-storey accommodation block some 300 yards long, hall, chapel, lodge and isolation unit is best appreciated from the air. Completed in 1872 at a cost of £90,579, the complex also included a farm and ancillary buildings and, at one time, its own gas-producing plant. As well as providing accommodation for up to 790 children, the residential school was one of Ashford's biggest employers, with up to 150 staff to care for the children and maintain the site. The choice of Ashford meant that a level greenfield site in Middlesex with reasonable transport links to the metropolis could be provided for the pauper children resident in the West London parishes of Paddington, Fulham and St. George's Square. Changing social conditions caused a gradual diminution in the numbers cared for here and by the time of its closure in 1955 only 40 children were being cared for. The subsequent and contentious arrival of detention and remand facilities at the site has an interesting precedent when, in 1855, the Middlesex Magistrates were proposing to establish a criminal reformatory school in Ashford. The photograph of the dining hall taken in 1946 gives some impression of the scale of the provision at Christmas. Although this was clearly a special occasion, it would seem that the residents enjoyed a healthy diet, the grounds of 70 acres also producing a variety of fresh produce as well as providing practical experience of horticulture and animal husbandry. A poem in the school magazine in 1934:

"We have roast meat or stew and milk puddings too.
Tomatoes and haricot beans.
And although for the most part we like all these things
We could very well do without greens."

WOODTHORPE ROAD SCHOOL c. 1909

Although photographer James Freeman of Coleridge Road seems to have issued very few postcards, his view of the new Woodthorpe Road School provides an excellent record of the now-vanished complex. Officially opened on 7th June, 1909, by the Chairman of the Middlesex County Council, the school – one of three local educational establishments started by the County in that decade – exemplified the major drive to provide schooling facilities for the burgeoning population of the area. Built to a design of the County Architect, Mr. Crothall, the building was to provide accommodation for 200 "mixed" scholars and 120 infants in classrooms grouped around a central hall. These were heated with open fires and lit by incandescent gas mantles. Part of the original design called for a "manual centre" for 20 boy pupils together with a "cooking centre" for 18 girls. The total cost of Ashford's new school was said to be £6,006. Its builders were the local firm of Thomas John Hawkins of Victoria Street, Westminster and Woodthorpe Road, Ashford. (see P.59)

WOODTHORPE ROAD SCHOOL, 1945

Following the First World War reorganisation of some local schools, Clarendon Road re-opened as a junior mixed school on 1st May, 1916, the senior children going to Woodthorpe Road. Further pressure on school capacity meant that, by 1931, "temporary" wooden classrooms were transferred here from another Middlesex County Council establishment, All Saints' School, Friern Barnet. Wartime education between 1939-1945 was disrupted for many by frequent air raid warnings, the shelters for the school being erected on the playing field further up the road acquired in 1938. Here the children would still receive education in the form of quizzes, singing and learning multiplication tables. This group of 45 boys taken c. 1945, possibly for Empire Day, 24th May, includes, top row, far left, John Armstrong. Also noticeable is the significant number of pupils who were members of the many uniformed organisations of the time, which were sponsored in the main by the various denominations. Further reorganisation led to the closure of the school in 1989, the remaining pupils transferring to Hengrove School to create Ashford Park School.

WOODTHORPE ROAD, 1912

A card issued by Edward Nicholson illustrates the major event of the laying of the foundation stone of the new church dedicated to St. Hilda. This ceremony, on 25th May, 1912, was performed by the Bishop of Kensington, John Maud, seen here on the left accompanied by Rev. Prebendary Prosser, the Rural Dean, and in the centre, Rev. Thornton, Vicar of Ashford 1900-1923, who was so instrumental in the establishment of the church. The architect John Samuel Alders (1847-1919) had many commissions from within the Diocese of London and his work was distinguished by a masterly handling of light and space. Another of his designs, St. George's Headstone, Pinner View, Harrow, is very similar and, like St. Hilda's, included a tower in the original design. Ashford's plans also included provision for an adjacent vicarage but in the event neither of these features was built. The nave and aisles were completed by 1913 when the Bishop of London, Arthur Winnington Ingram, dedicated the structure on 17th April 1913. Following the hiatus caused by the First World War, the Chancel, Vestry and Lady Chapel were completed and the Church consecrated on St. Hilda's day, 17th November, 1928.

Church Parade. 10th Middlesex. Ashford.   W.H.A.4165.

STANWELL ROAD, 1914

Members of the de Salis family were involved in many aspects of local life. They included Cecil, County Councillor for Stanwell and Alderman for Middlesex 1899-1937, and William Fane de Salis, living at "Woodthorpe", West District Road in 1914: both were heavily involved with the Territorial Army. Whether this proximity had any influence over the location of the newly-arrived Territorials at the end of November 1914 is not clear: however, the large Church Hall, billeting facilities, open ground and nearby railway were no doubt all considerations in the choice of the area for the Battalion of 999 men. Another card shows the troops being addressed by their Commanding Officer, Lt.-Col. C.R. Johnson, somewhere in the vicinity of the West District School. The corrugated iron hall, opened in January 1908, was later used as a food depot in both World Wars, burnt down in 1967 and was replaced by the present structure. Also seen is the wooden buttressing at the end of the church marking the state of the construction at the outbreak of war in August 1914.

CENTRAL ASHFORD, 1929

Further evidence of the value of the aerial photograph is seen in this view published by the Woodthorpe Road newsagent George Rose. On the left can be seen the layout of the extensive allotments now occupied by West Close. Plot rents were paid to the railway authorities and it is presumed that this holding adjacent to the track was part of the land bought up by the London & South Western Railway Company in the 1840s. Activity on these areas fluctuated considerably with national and international events. Both World Wars saw a massive up-take for additional non-rationed food production – the added benefits of physical exercise and the mainly organic produce being an underestimated advantage! By the early 1960s the area was largely derelict – an effect of changing leisure habits and the major disturbance caused by the construction of the Southampton-London Airport fuel pipeline. On the other side of Woodthorpe Road, the recently completed St. Hilda's and its associated church hall remain the dominant feature of this part of the town.

BLERIOT AIRCRAFT, 12th March, 1911

Evidence that Edward Nicholson was working seven days a week is seen here. The Middlesex Chronicle's report helps to explain why this Blériot monoplane was photographed at Ashford. "Whilst flying from the Hendon Aerodrome to Brooklands on Saturday Mr. Greswell, driving (sic) a Blériot monoplane, lost his way in the fog and descended on the Payne, Trappes estate near Ashford Station. Arrangements were made at once to safeguard the machine and on Sunday Mr. Greswell resumed his interrupted flight." This incident, only two years after the inaugural cross-Channel flight, allowed the photographer to record the take-off on Sunday, the slow speed of the machine and the skill of Mr. Nicholson helping to create this crisp image of the event. Perhaps Ashfordians were used to the new transport system, with regular low-level flights between the new facilities at Hendon (opened by Claude Grahame-White in 1910) and Brooklands (first flight 1907, flying schools established 1910). Mr. C.H. Greswell gained his flying certificate on 15th November, 1910 at the Grahame-White Flying School at Brooklands.

ASHFORD.
March 12th 1911.

STATION CRESCENT c. 1934

By the mid-1930s the suburbanisation of Ashford was in full swing. However, the area, only recently taken under the full administrative control of Staines Urban District Council, was still evolving the now ubiquitous facilities of street lighting, paved roads and mains drainage. The frontagers of the recently completed Station Crescent, along with those of St. Hilda's Avenue and Wellington Road, were involved in a dispute with the local authority as to the cost of the work to provide proper road surfaces and footpaths. One resident was even moved to suggest that the question was the biggest thing Ashford had ever known! A compromise involving reducing the width of the new reinforced concrete roads was reached, saving the householders 3s. per foot on the cost, Station Crescent noted as being 4 ft. wider than the others. By May 1935 the road was being made up; however, a fierce fire in the road in June of that year revealed that the Brigade had difficulty with the water supply from the existing hydrants and utilised water from a ditch. By the end of July the street was made up and taken over as a public highway.

STANWELL ROAD c. 1913

As well as commissioning his own photographs, William Applebee (see p. 23) also seems to have taken over the glass plate archive of the Teddington postcard publisher Young & Co. and re-numbered the images. The history of the area illustrated, part of the Gloucester Villas development of the 1860s, has been the subject of the excellent publication "Gordon Road Estate" by Mary Mason. The group of smartly dressed boys were residents of the Boys' Home, part of the Staines Union facility in the London Road later used as the nurses' home and now demolished and replaced by Ashford Hospital. The children, aged 5 to13, attended the new Woodthorpe Road School by arrangement with the Managers who in turn invoiced the Guardians of the Union for their education. Coincidentally, the children are pictured adjacent to "The Laurels", home to the eponymous private day school from 1934 to 1943. Its original Principal, Miss K. D. E. Trapps, was advertising a Kindergarten and Preparatory school for boys here, the owner of the house, Mrs. H.K. Gebbett, applying to erect a building for use as a schoolroom in 1938.

ABBOTSFORD SCHOOL, STANWELL ROAD, 1959

Graham Smeed's talent for photography was evident when, as a pupil, he recorded this group of teaching staff and Headmaster Mr. G. Ibbotson from the boys' section of Abbotsford School, taken in the quadrangle in the summer of 1959. The school owes its existence to the need of the Middlesex County Council to provide "elementary" education in the area in the 1930s. The Authority agreed to acquire this strategically placed site of originally c. 11½ acres in 1935. Work on the new complex was largely completed at the onset of war in 1939, a new County Library, Clinic and Education Offices also opening at this time. Although occupied by Army Infantry Records during the War, such was the pressure on school accommodation that boys were taught here, including some from Echelford, which was heavily overcrowded. Post-war, from January 1947 the campus became the home of the Stanwell Road Secondary Modern School for Boys, Head. Capt. A.W. Robertson; and the Stanwell Road Secondary Modern School for Girls, Headmistress. Miss Wills. formerly acting Head of Woodthorpe Road School. Some of the staff of the boys' school seen here had been on active service and entered the profession via the post-war training scheme for teachers. Conditions for staff and pupils alike were difficult – the great efforts made to manure the ground for the magnificent shrubs in the quadrangle and the cannibalisation of car batteries for lead to use in metalworking are remembered! In 1958 the joint school underwent a name change, reputedly at the suggestion of Miss Wills: the new name linked the Abbot of St. Peter's, Westminster and the ford of the Ash to give "Abbotsford". In 1975 it became a comprehensive school for 1,140 pupils, a system said to give pupils and parents the best of grammar and secondary modern education. Further changes occurred in September 1987, when the school re-opened as Ashford High School, and again in September 2004 when it became the Ash Technology College.

15

WELSH GIRLS' SCHOOL, 1926

The visit of the Prince of Wales to Ashford on 14th July, 1926, was on the occasion of the laying of the foundation stone of a new gymnasium at the Welsh Girls' School. A crowd of about 500 together with pupils and staff witnessed the Prince performing the ceremony accompanied by the Very Reverend Dean Brownrigg, Chaplain to the school; Sir Frederick Kenyon, Keeper of the British Museum; and the Right Reverend Bishop Watkin Williams, Treasurer of the Most Honourable and Loyal Society of Ancient Britons. Loyalty to the new Hanoverian Dynasty was manifest when the Society was formed in 1714 and Royal patronage ensued. A charity school was established in Grays Inn Road, London, in 1718 for the purpose of boarding, clothing and educating 80 boys and 25 girls born of Welsh parents in or within 10 miles of London and not having a parochial settlement within these limits. The new campus at Ashford was opened by Queen Victoria's consort, Prince Albert, on 13th July, 1857. Further royal patronage occurred in November 1898 when the chapel, dedicated in 1897 to St. David, was visited by the Duchess of Albany, widow of Queen Victoria's youngest son.

ST. DAVID'S LIBRARY c. 1968

Pictured by Mr. William Howlett, one of Ashford's longest-standing photographic specialists, pupils were recorded studying in the school's library. Prior to its planned evacuation to Wales in the summer of 1939, the school housed a unique collection of printed material related to the Welsh language and history, bequeathed to the school in 1783. Much of this material and the archives of the Society of Ancient Britons from 1718 were then placed in the care of the National Library of Wales. The school had been planning major improvements prior to the war, including the installation of a hot water system, improved dormitory arrangements and new science, geography and music rooms. Apart from the provision of hot water and the erection of hutments for the use of its wartime occupants, the military and civilian personnel of the Army Pay Corps, these and many other improvements awaited the School's return to its Ashford campus in 1946 from wartime evacuation at Powys Castle. A further royal occasion commemorating the centenary of its arrival here occurred on 21st November, 1957, when Princess Margaret visited. In September 1968 the Welsh Girls' School changed its name to St. David's.

WOODTHORPE ROAD AND CLARENDON ROAD, 1928

Aerial photography provides the ideal record of a moment in time – in this case the area around the station and Woodthorpe Road. Goods yards on both up and down platforms are well used, with stabling for the horses working from here until c. 1955 on the down side. The line itself would soon be electrified and opened for faster passenger traffic from 6th July, 1930, the up platform extended and a new signal box opened in the same year. Just beyond, and perhaps best appreciated from above, is the now landscaped and developed area of the still-active rubbish shoot. Other significant industrial activities can also be seen in the area still zoned for industry, including the Woodthorpe Joinery Co. Sherwood Cottage, a large detached residence fronted by poplar trees, still stood on the corner of Clarendon Road and Woodthorpe Road, its strategic site to be occupied by a parade of shops and flats by 1935. Also best seen from the air, the site of the original Methodist Church erected in 1899 by Chertsey builder T. J. Knight at a cost of £1,160 and its associated buildings is well illustrated, including the Wesley Hall, a re-used military building erected here in 1921 and used by a number of organisations including contingents of the Boys' and Girls' Brigades and the County Council, who ran maternity and child welfare clinics here; and the Band Room, erected c. 1907. Familiar features yet to appear on the railway embankment were the tobacconist's kiosk started in 1934 by the blind Mr. F. Perkins and the advertising hoardings erected by the mid-1950s.

"UP" PLATFORM c. 1905

Although the mainly London-bound commuters could have been photographed at any time during the past 158 years, this Edwardian scene provides much distinctly contemporary detail. Indeed, the rush and crush of travelling Ashfordians at this time were much photographed and a variety of postcards issued, illustrating in particular the popularity of the so-called "workmen's tickets" which provided for cheaper travel before 8.00 am. The rise of Ashford as a commuter town was inexorable once the late 19th-century building boom got under way. Indeed, the particulars and map for the Ashford Estate issued c. 1890 give details of the railway timetable for prospective new residents, with 14 trains per day to London listed. By 1934 on the newly electrified line no fewer than 46 trains a day were timetabled en route to Waterloo. Also recorded for posterity were the goods shed and office, a wagon loading gauge and the gas lighting on the platforms at a time when there was not a single public street light in the town. Mr. Hoad, who settled in Ashford in 1908, recalled being impressed by the well-cultivated flower beds at the back end of the up line and flowers and foliage hiding the goods yard at the rear! Commuters more than half a century later were, however, still using the Edwardian facilities including the rolling stock, complaints being made in 1949 that the carriages were fifty-year-old ex-South Eastern and Chatham railway stock.

STATION YARD c. 1980

The area once occupied by the up goods yards and sidings has an interesting history of use and re-use over the past 150 years. Part of the land opposite the new Welsh Girls' School, "the water hole", was purchased in 1856 and utilised as the school's rubbish tip. By c. 1890 the extent of the quarrying in the area adjacent to the station is indicated on the new Ashford Estate plan (centrefold). The object of this work was the gravel and sand beneath the thin topsoil and brick earth. Prior to the introduction of mechanical extraction, hand digging was the norm. Once flooded or worked out, the land had value as one of the parish dumps or "shoots". Photographs of the goods yard of c. 1905 show the area now back-filled and occupied by the yards and stores of builders' merchants. One consequence of the backfilling with "nitrogenous matter" (among other things) was the later lush growth of brambles, nettles and deadly nightshade. By c. 1980, part of the plot occupied by the recycled land was in turn used for motor salvage.

ASHFORD STATION c. 1910

The original buildings, a halt created for the opening of the London and South Western Railways line in 1848, seem to have been rebuilt, reputedly for the arrival of Prince Albert to open the nearby Welsh School in 1857, although a plan exists of "Ashford New Station" dated September 1871. At this time the population of Ashford was still largely focused around the Parish Church and mainly involved in agriculture. The enormous growth in population connected with the building of "New Ashford" and the rise of the commuter meant that the station was the focus of tremendous activity, with goods yards on both up and down lines, a resident Station Master and his family, a number of coal and builders' depots, a parcel and luggage service to the metropolis and beyond and the bookstall of W.H. Smith, opened on 24th June, 1896. Also available was a wide range of consumer facilities in the immediate vicinity, including a taxi rank and a post office offering a multiple collection and delivery service.

STATION APPROACH c. 1920

Another local postcard publisher was the Gresham Photographic Co. of Chertsey, who were active in this area following the end of the First World War. This view was one of the most frequently photographed aspects of Ashford, the adjacent post office no doubt being one factor. The handcart delivery system of Barnes Stores at 13-15 Station Approach and perambulators using the open road are suggestive of the road conditions of the time, although the parked cars and taxis by the station hint at things to come. The area around the station, richly provided with a variety of retailers and services, has always been notable for the absence of any form of "on" licensed premises. In fact, Ashford seems to stand alone in this regard compared with other stations on the line and although the "Royal Hart" is relatively close, the lack of a Station Hotel or even a beerhouse is worthy of note. The promoters of the New Ashford estate had in fact marked out the area now occupied by the Station Road/Station Approach/Woodthorpe Road triangle as a site for a hotel or public building. Teetotal visitors to Edwardian Ashford also had the facilities of a temperance hotel in Woodthorpe Road, address unknown.

DENNIS CESS COLLECTOR
c. 1928

One drawback of the area's very rapid development was the lack of mains drainage for the rapidly expanding population, which had grown from 2,700 in 1891 to 8,719 in 1931. The local authority collected both household rubbish and sewage. In 1910, for example, the authority had dealt with 2,554 cubic yards of new refuse and 1½ million gallons of sewage from 1,715 cesspools in the Ashford area. The household rubbish was shot into worked-out gravel pits, the contents of cesspools taken to sites in the Clockhouse Lane and Feltham Hill Road areas, some of the expense to the ratepayers being recouped by the sale of cabbages grown at the sewage beds. The tenants and owners of the parade, "Bon Marche", experienced typical problems, with complaints about smells and the general inconvenience of a regular (or irregular) collection. In 1914 a new "vacuum exhauster" was purchased for emptying cesspools and in 1928 the local council bought this 1,200-gallon "motor cesspool emptier" for £1,500 from the specialist Guildford makers, Dennis.

WOODTHORPE ROAD, 1916

Weather conditions of all types provided a rich source of subject matter for the postcard publisher, this view of a snowfall in February 1916 being a typical example of the genre. Its subject, Smyth's Stores, was a general store and sub-post office opened in 1892 when the trees, thought to be limes, were also planted. These survived the demolition of the building in 1929, by which time they had been formed into an attractive espalier, but had been cut down by c. 1935. The building contained a basement utilised for the storage of paraffin also retailed by Mr. Smyth via a tricycle, a reminder of the days when the fuel was widely used for domestic lighting. However, the smell of the volatile material permeating the shop above provided an abiding memory for some! The window display prominently features postcards, perhaps the work of Mr. Applebee and others. Around 1905 Mr. Smyth had published his own series of cards featuring his premises, the station and many other local scenes, some of which feature on the front cover.

WOODTHORPE ROAD c. 1923

A summer day c. 1923 captured by the Applebee Company provides more evidence of contemporary retailing. On the left at no. 2, Alfred Johnson's fishmonger's operated from the building previously occupied by the Grimsby Fish Supply Company and later by MacFisheries. Shoppers could also check the quality of the produce on offer – fish, poultry and probably kippers in the wooden boxes – for themselves before the now ubiquitous packaging and health and safety legislation. This feature was not without its problems: an Ashford fishmonger complained in 1926 about road metalling thrown up during tarmacadaming of the road. The next-door premises of Ambrose C. Rose also had a long history as a newsagent and tobacconist and for a short period following the closure of Smyth's Stores c. 1929 as a sub-post office. A number of local postcards were also published at this time with Mr. Rose's imprint. No. 6, the premises of Albert Baker advertising Luncheon and Teas, was also noted as "ham and beef stores". Later occupants Frank Clinton and family also carried on this tradition: famous for faggots and pease pudding, a takeaway enjoyed by many including the author in the mid-1950s.

WOODTHORPE ROAD, 1936

William Craswell's new "Central Garage" opened in 1936, bringing together his mechanical and horticultural enterprises. Members of Frederick Craswell's family had been established in Woodthorpe Road since at least 1912, listed variously as corn dealers and timber merchants. In 1920 his son William is recorded as a cycle maker working at the rear of the store and by 1930 as a corn dealer. The construction of the new building catering for the ever-increasing vehicle trade was recorded in a series of photographs including the delivery of a large fuel tank, presumably still in situ. Its accompanying pump, seen here, is a reminder of the days when fuel was routinely available at the kerbside. Post war, Mr. Craswell's other business was eventually taken over by Mr. B. Ramsden, remembered as an avuncular supplier of a wide range of horticultural and avian specialities. His son Peter, under the imprint of Aspen Books, published a number of titles covering histories of the local fire brigades, compilations of local views and a history of the town to 1940.

WOODTHORPE ROAD c. 1930

The wide roadway and pavement in this part of Woodthorpe Road is a reminder of the Victorian development of this part of Ashford connected with the gradual sale of the Ashford Ford Estate. An agreement dated 1st July, 1868, between J.L. Wood, Thomas Smith, James Mason and James Mann, who was about to lay out building ground, also included provision for the adjacent road and footpaths. The carriageway was to be 50 ft. wide, fitted in all respects for the traffic of men and carriages and other vehicles drawn by horses. It was to have a footpath 10 ft. wide on both sides and a level foundation, an 8-in. layer of good gravel and a 4-in. layer of good sound gravel from which all the hoggins had been sifted: the footpaths to have gravel surfaces and all necessary drains and cesspools bounded by a fir fence with posts nine feet apart with two rails and a standard. Reasonable street lighting was to wait for nearly 50 years. The estate seems to have given rise to the appellation "New Ashford" – one of the first mentions of this occurs in a directory of 1874.

WOODTHORPE ROAD, 1935

In 1935 the whole of the United Kingdom and the British Empire celebrated the Silver Jubilee of the accession of King George V. Events large and small were arranged to commemorate this auspicious occasion and Ashford's many organisations joined in with the national enthusiasm. Seen here are members of the 2nd Ashford Girls' Life Guards en route to the service of thanksgiving held at St. Hilda's Church on 6th May 1935. The Girls' Life Brigade was affiliated to the Congregational Church and was formed in England in 1902 with the motto: "To Save Life", and the aim of helping and encouraging girls to become responsible, self-reliant Christian women. The special circumstances of the occasion, permitting safe pedestrian passage, are in marked contrast to the regular dangers at this dangerous junction at the time. Ever-increasing road traffic and a growing accident toll led the council in the same year to commence negotiations with the Southern Railway company, Charles Adamson and Messrs. Purveys with a view to acquiring the land needed to improve the sight lines. A footpath from Station Crescent to Woodthorpe Road was also discussed.

CHAUCER ROAD c. 1936

One of Ashford's more unusual private educational establishments was the Ardross Kennels, established in Chaucer Road c. 1923 by Mrs. Marie Beamish-Levey. By the mid-1930s the establishment had grown considerably and occupied nos. 2, 4, 8, 10, 12, 22, 7, 9 and 11 Chaucer Road. Here pedigree Airedale terriers were bred and kennelled with the help of up to 20 girls who trained in kennel management and grooming. The animals were exported all over the world and a teacher was also employed for the benefit of the overseas students amongst them. Occasional problems with dangerous dogs and noise pollution led to documentation of further details of the school, which in 1933 was said to maintain between 18 and 50 animals here. Summoned in 1935 by near neighbour Charles Adamson, Mrs. Beamish-Levey stated that the dogs were only troublesome in August when the kennel maids went on holiday. The mass exercising of the animals was a familiar sight in the mid 1930s: a contemporary report records a "regiment of young women marching along in masterly style".

WOLSEY ROAD c. 1911

Another of the residential streets developed around the turn of the 19th/20th century, Wolsey Road has a particular claim to fame in connection with the photographic history of Ashford. "Woodbine", a semi-detached house, was the home of one of the South of England's most important and prolific publishers of topographical photographic postcards, William Henry Applebee. His invoices show him established here by May 1911, and that his specialities were "Photographic Local View Post Card Albums and Revolving Stands". Applebee's output was prodigious. This card is marked W.H.A.2. and, although not postally used, may well be one of his very earliest Ashford publications: another version numbered 1919 is known using the same negative. Although William died early in 1915 aged 30, the business seems to have been carried on by his widow Lucy Annie and on the evidence of the cards appears to have continued producing high-quality view postcards until c. 1928. Views of many areas of the Thames Valley were photographed with numbering of the photographic archive reaching at least 6,250.

WolseyRoad. Ashford.   W.H.A.2.

CHESTERFIELD ROAD c. 1913 & c. 1920

Two card views published by the William Applebee firm from c. 1913 and c. 1920 looking east and west provide further evidence of the value of the postcard in recording the contemporary environment. Apart from the lack of motorised traffic, these street scenes again reveal subtle details of period conditions, including the apparent total lack of homes with telephones, the minimal street lighting and the delivery of milk from one of Ashford's dairy enterprises. Churn-based milk deliveries were a twice-daily event prior to the advent of affordable refrigerators: a report of 1916, however, records the theft in Chesterfield Road of bottled milk supplied by Marshall's Dairy of Station Road. The road itself was the subject of concern for the local authority over many years. In 1911 the footpaths of the long thoroughfare were put in order and its use as bypass during the reconstruction of the Ford Bridge in 1921 caused damage to the roadway. This occasioned the Council to refer to documentation of 1836 as to their liability to repair the route. In 1904, however, Ashford's Parish Council was asking the District Authority to take over and repair the continuation of the road at its western end, i.e. the footpath alongside the West District School. Intriguingly, this alignment, heading towards the known Roman occupation at the Bronzefield Prison and Hengrove Farm sites, was known as the "Old Green Lane", a place name often associated with Roman roads and possibly suggesting the true origins of Chesterfield Road.

VOLUNTEERS 1915

This cheerful group of volunteer soldiers illustrates the composition
of the army at the outset of the First World War. The postcard
produced from the photograph was posted on 3rd March, 1915, and is
addressed from Gordon Villa, Chesterfield Road. Its message to "Dear
Mother" from "Wilfred" includes the line: "We haven't had any news
about our transfer. At present it doesn't seem it will come off."
Assuming that the author was one of the group, perhaps billeted in
Chesterfield Road, the lack of censorship of these local mails is
interesting. These newly arrived Territorial troops in Staines and
Ashford were, according to contemporary reports, "heartily welcomed
and that there had been hardly a case where householders have not
been eager to house some of the men who are prepared to defend their
country from invasion if the necessity arises". The 2/10 Battalion of
the Middlesex Regiment was formed at their depot in Stamford Brook
in September 1914 and was attached to the 2nd Brigade. By July
1915 these men and boys were in action in the ill-fated Gallipoli
campaign and suffered many casualties.

ARLINGTON ROAD c. 1946

Although communities around the country organised more or less ad
hoc celebrations to commemorate the end of the war in Europe in
May 1945 locally, "official" celebrations were arranged the following
year which enabled many demobilised service personnel and
ex-prisoners of war to participate. Staines Urban District Council
events planned for 8th June 1946 were affected by inclement weather,
although Ashford's Wards did not participate in this and held a
massive celebration of their own at the Clockhouse Lane recreation
ground on 22nd June, 1946. However, the residents of Arlington and
Springfield Roads and part of Chesterfield Road held their own
Victory parties in celebration of the peace and home-coming of local
servicemen. A VJ party was organised by a committee in September
1945 with a day-long programme of entertainment, including races
and games for the children and dancing in the evening for the adults.
The following year some 300 residents including 90 children took
part in the festivities, which carried on until midnight. As seen here,
the children enjoyed the tea, comprising jellies, trifles, cakes, etc., that
followed a sports programme including running games and thread-
the-needle. All the guests were given paper hats, the boys and girls
also receiving gifts of sweets, knitting bags, beakers or toy rabbits.
The adults later enjoyed singing and dancing in the road until
midnight, aided by four spotlights. Planning for the event had begun
the previous August and was aided by a "1d a week" fund, which had
raised nearly £50 to fund the festivities.

THE LINKS c. 1930 and c. 1965

"Gone but not forgotten", a familiar epitaph for many departed hostelries, perhaps never seemed so appropriate as for the Links Hotel, demolished in 1985. The present excellent establishment on the site represents recent architectural styling and function as much as the original structure was a product of a "land of hope and glory" and brewers' self-aggrandisement. The story of The Links, so well illustrated in Barry Dix's 1990 publication "Ashford Past and Present", provides a timely reminder that investment in the leisure industry has always been problematic!

Architectural fashion at the turn of the 19th/20th century decreed that towers and a cupola were among the "must have" features of prominent new builds. The Links' copper sheathed cupola has at least survived and is now serving a similar purpose on a large residence in Virginia, U.S.A, its size and weight apparently having proved too much for a new home locally. The Ford Bridge/Links crossroads was also home to another strategically placed establishment, the "FifeHead" garage and one-time stables of J. Simons. Also seen in this aerial view is another of the K3 telephone kiosks placed here in 1930 and the original stopping point for the London Transport route 117 and Green Line coaches. Although the hotel facilities offered by The Links proved less successful, the other amenities available here were well used, with ballroom and other dancing, a snooker club and meetings of a number of other local organisations. The various bars were also well patronised, the interior view in the 1960s giving a valuable insight into the ambience and style of the period.

MANOR ROAD c. 1914

Another consequence of the sale of the Ashford Manor estate was the rapid development of a number of roads in the immediate vicinity of the new links. In 1902 the Ashford Manor Estate and Golf Club Ltd. began selling building plots in Fordbridge and Manor Roads. As well as owning four of the properties in the newly constructed road, builder Herbert George Wallage also lived in "Knapton", Manor Road. The development was not without its problems and a contemporary report illustrates how the local authority, including a number of councillors who were also developers, were not afraid to uphold the regulations then in force. In February 1904, builder Mr. Dooley was served notice to pull down two houses he was building here on the grounds of their bad construction, the District Surveyor also taking out proceedings against him. By the time of this Applebee postcard the road was well established, with the almost ubiquitous home delivery of a local trader.

FORDBRIDGE ROAD c. 1935

The earliest reliable large-scale maps of the area show that by 1865, apart from Ford Farm, there were no houses in the road: by 1895, however, there were 14 and by 1914, 52 properties. Some of these new larger residences were home to a number of private schools also springing up at this time. At one time Ford Bridge Road was contemporaneously home to three of these establishments: Cranfant Lodge established here c. 1914; St. Cyr's; and Sheen College, originally based in "Manor View". A number of these schools, as well as educating local children, also advertised boarding facilities. In 1930, plans for a new County elementary school for up to 500 children in the Fontmell Park Road area, which would have involved access from Percy Road, were abandoned in favour of the Knapp Road site. In 1937 the rising tide of redevelopment occasioned residents of the neighbourhood to petition the local authority against re-zoning a portion of the road but in favour of retaining the original scheme for six houses to an acre and not nine, which would affect the value of all the properties in the road.

FORDBRIDGE ROAD, 1958

Following the clearing of the debt on the Feltham Road site, a new Catholic church was planned and the prominent site in Fordbridge Road purchased in 1925. St. Michael's was designed by Sir Giles Gilbert Scott, architect of Battersea and Bankside Power Stations and Liverpool Cathedral. His drawings were exhibited at the Royal Academy in 1927, Sir Giles considering St. Michael's one of his most successful churches. Work started in the same year, Cardinal Bourne laying the foundation stone, and by 1930 the funding had enabled the south aisle and two chapels to be built. Father Edwin Owen intended to add a little to the building every year until completion. Wartime setbacks included roof damage caused by the nearby impact of a V2 and the death of Father Owen, both in October 1944. His mother, who died c. 1941, was also heavily involved in the work of the parish: the tabernacle and statue of St. Michael were among her many gifts, she and her son placing their entire private income at the church's disposal. The final phase of construction began in 1958, the early Romanesque-style church being consecrated by Cardinal Godfrey in 1960.

PRINCES ROAD c. 1930

Another of the streets laid out during the development of New Ashford is Princes Road, as seen in this view published as part of the WHL series of Ashford scenes. Two features of the road not visible here were a shop and a Brethren Meeting House. The shop, at Westcroft, no. 24 Princes Road, was run by Henry Nash and is listed here between 1911 and 1935. Mr. Nash specialised in repairing china and glass by riveting and also in re-caning chairs. Noted on the map of the area of c. 1890 (see centrefold), the Brethren building was reported to be of wood and corrugated iron with interior fittings including coconut matting and an iron stove. The Brethren movement began in Dublin in the late 1820s and, as a Christian group, felt that the Established Church had become too involved with secular life and had abandoned many of the basic truths of Christianity. The available documentation and memories suggest that the adherents who met here were "Open" to the wider community rather than "Exclusive": however, following the burning down of the chapel on November 10th, 1944, there is no further mention of the local group.

AN ASHFORD RAPPER GROUP, CLARENDON ROAD SCHOOL, c. 1910

A number of photographic postcards exist illustrating the wide range of educational and theatrical activity on offer to the pupils of Clarendon Road a century ago. Here, children are seen participating in the Edwardian revival of all forms of English folk dance, which manifested itself in schools nationwide with country and Maypole dancing much in evidence. The sword or rapper dance was a Northumbrian and Durham tradition recorded by Cecil Sharp, one of the major figures in the folk dance movement. Its adaptation for children, along with drilling and marching, was an exercise in teaching coordination and teamwork. The lack of a playing field at the school was perhaps not such an obvious disadvantage, with relatively safe streets and nearby open land on which to play. The new school was also very much a community facility, with organisations such as the Ashford & District Smallholders' Club, the Juvenile Swimming Club, the Parish Council, the Ashford Literary & Debating Society and political groups, among others, using the hall for evening meetings in the years before the First World War.

CLARENDON ROAD c. 1930

Even after the passage of more than three quarters of a century and the loss of the school buildings on the left, the vista, *sans* motor traffic, is still recognisable. Home delivery – in this case of milk – can be seen, but apart from the young driver, a complete lack of other transport. The growth of telephone ownership in the community and the increased provision of street lighting are also evident. The present disposition of streetlights is often based on their original strategic position, as seen here, adjacent to a school and a church. Almost directly opposite the school at no. 94 was the home of Miss Lily Taylor, a fondly remembered infant teacher who retired in 1947. In 1948 the education authority gave the school electric lighting and replaced the heating system, which had given so much trouble during the harsh winter of the previous year. School toilets, the subject of so many memories for pupils, were also a problem for the staff at this time. The County Council reported that the sanitary accommodation for eleven teachers and nine canteen staff consisted of one W.C. and one basin without hot water.

Band of the 10th Middx. Regiment, Ashford. 1915.
4128 W.H.A. Copyright.

BAND OF THE 10th MIDDLESEX REGIMENT, FORD ROAD, 1915

Postmarked 21st January, 1915, the original caption on this postcard, dating it to that year, demonstrates the speed with which postcard publishers could turn their wares around. William Henry Applebee's company, based nearby in Wolsey Road, had within days of exposing the photographic plate produced a card for sale. Applebee's target audience would be patriotic local residents and members of the regiment and its band, shown drumming up support for their unit and the war effort. The arrival of a large body of homesick troops eager to correspond with family and friends no doubt greatly boosted the demand for picture postcards of the area. Other cards are known showing the same group in Station Approach and outside the Links Hotel. Each battalion in the British Army at this time had 16 Privates who rated as stretcher-bearers and were also the band's musicians with fifes, drums and bugles. During their sojourn in Ashford, however, the battalion developed a larger band and gave open-air concerts to large gatherings at the then open land at the junction of Chaucer and Clarendon Roads.

CLARENDON ROAD, 1944

Although Ashford escaped much of the damage inflicted by the Luftwaffe on other areas of the country, by 1944 new and indiscriminate weapons were unleashed on Britain, causing much damage and loss of life, especially in the South East, with London being the principal target of the Nazis. The cause of the devastation seen here was the impact of a V2 "rocket bomb" which fell on the corner of Dudley Road on Saturday morning, 28th October, 1944, causing the death of three residents. These rockets, the second of Hitler's "Vengeance" weapons, were first fired at England on 8th September, 1944, the last falling at Orpington, Kent, on 28th March, 1945. As well as the damage caused at the point of impact, the V2 rocket created an earthquake effect over a wider area. Cracks in a wall in Clarendon Road 300 yards away were said to have been caused by this incident. The impact of one of the first V1 "flying bombs" in Poplar Road on 16th June, 1944 also caused widespread destruction, including eight homes damaged beyond repair and the loss of two lives.

CLARENDON ROAD, 1913

The reason for the siting of the Clarendon Cinema in a sedate back street remains uncertain: however, this image records Ashford's latest facility. The brainchild of Thomas Perrin, a builder from Slough, a licence for a "Cinema Theatre" in Clarendon Road had been granted to him by Middlesex County Council on 13th November, 1910, the local authority also gave the "Clarendon Cinema Company" permission to build a "motor house" in March 1911. Distinctive original features include the exterior gas lighting essential for the evening performances, the box office and the first floor projection room. The terracotta ball finials, a contemporary architectural flourish, were also seen on the Fire Station and the Clarendon Road School. The billboard, which advertises a newsreel covering the wedding of Prince Arthur of Connaught and the Duchess of Fife on 15th October, 1913, dates this view. Cinemas were springing up all over the world at this time: Ashford's venue was not the first locally, as a converted hall in Thames Street, Staines – The Palace – and purpose-built cinemas in Feltham and Egham had all opened by 1910.

CLARENDON ROAD c. 1927

By c. 1923 the Clarendon Cinema's frontage had been revamped with the addition of a façade of minarets and arabesque detailing reflecting the post-war enthusiasm for all things eastern or exotic coupled with ever-more-lavish Hollywood productions. The venue still offered Ashfordians a wide range of film attractions – both American imports and home-grown features. A contemporary advert. gives an insight into the conditions enjoyed by patrons. Seats were priced at 5d, 8d, 1/2d and 1/6d (approx. 2p – 7¹/₂p), with the promise of a "steady picture and no eye strain" and a happy family life with regular attendance! Bicycles were accommodated at the rear. By 1930 the cinema was screening "talkies" and as well as the changing weekly programme of films the building was occasionally used for concerts in aid of local charities. When the Perrin family's other cinema opened in Ashford, (see p. 46) this building became first a wartime "British Restaurant" offering cheap nutritious meals, which finally closed on the 31st March, 1947; then a National Insurance office; and later a depot for "Farley's Rusks" and egg distribution.

Leave WATERLOO.	Leave ASHFORD.
7.10 a.m.	7.49 a.m.
8. 0 „	8.15 „
9.38 „	8.25 „
10.45 „	9. 8 „
12.40 p.m.	9.24 „
2.10 „	10.14 „
3. 0 „	11.44 „
4.15 „	12.55 p.m.
4.55 „	3. 4 „
5.50 „	5. 1 „
6.37 „	5.54 „
8. 5 „	7.11 „
9. 5 „	8.56 „
10.10 „	10.59 „
11.10 „	...
12. 0 „	...

Plan of
ASHFORD
ASHFORD, MID
BELONGING TO M
FREEHOLD PLOTS TO

SOLD

FOOTPATH

PRINCES ROAD

ALBERT ROAD

DUDLEY ROAD

CHURCH ROAD

CLARENDO ROAD

CLARENDON ROAD

FORD BRIDGE ROAD

LONDON ROAD

ASHFORD VILLAGE

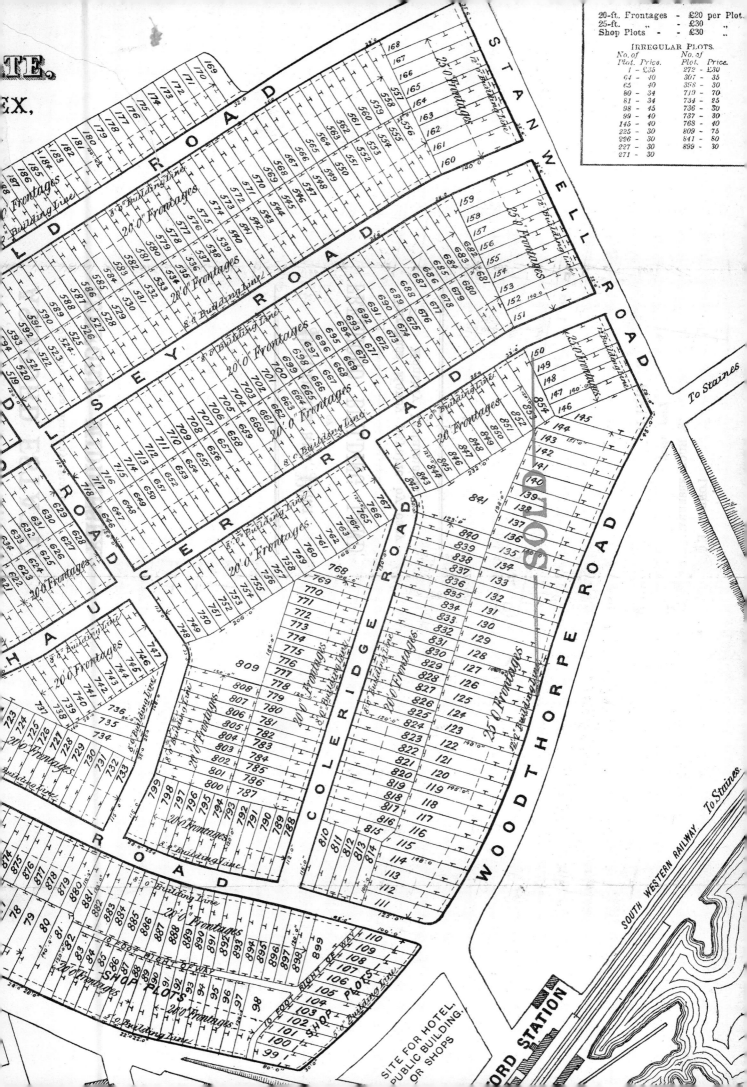

20-ft. Frontages	-	£20 per Plot
25-ft.	"	- £30 "
Shop Plots	"	- £30 "

IRREGULAR PLOTS.

No. of Plot.	Price.	No. of Plot.	Price.
1	£35	272	£30
64	40	307	35
65	40	358	30
80	34	719	70
81	34	734	25
98	45	736	30
99	40	737	30
145	40	768	40
225	30	809	75
226	30	841	80
227	30	899	30
271	30		

SITE FOR HOTEL, PUBLIC BUILDING, OR SHOPS

SOLD

To Staines

SOUTH WESTERN RAILWAY

To Staines

...FORD STATION

LOCK'S WORKSHOP c. 1950

Some of Ashford's oldest craft skills are maintained to this day by Lodge Bros., successors to Lock's as funeral directors at their premises in Clarendon Road. Seen here are Lock's craftsmen making and polishing bespoke coffins. The present firm was founded in Feltham in the late 18th century and took over Lock's in 1972, with the Chapels of Rest and workshops seen here established at the Clarendon Road site by c. 1900. The Lock Family were connected with the Primitive Methodist Church at Ashford Common from 1888 and later the new Wesleyan Church opposite. Typically, Lock's were also builders, with many of the skills interchangeable between the professions. As well as constructing the Clarendon Road Congregational Church in 1901, they were also responsible for a number of local house-building projects including houses and shops in Windmill Road in 1904 and a development of "semis" in 1930. Mr. Walter Lock died in 1930, the business then being carried on by his son. Mrs. Lock had another sideline in the form of a shop adjoining the premises which traded household goods and, convenient to the cinema, confectionery.

VILLAGE WAY c. 1936

Photographer Albert Bull neatly posed a Job's milk float with some of Ashford's new landmarks: the post office, Echelford School and the newly-built Village Way, advertised as "Ashford Garden Village, the Gem of West Middlesex". Dairy retailing was undergoing a transformation with the advent of larger groupings and chains, which took over the rounds and facilities of the older local firms. By 1937 Ashford was in the main served by three major concerns for door-to-door delivery: the Staines and District Co-Op, Herd & Clark and Job's, based in Hanworth. Job's had take over Herbert Cook's facilities at 12 Church Road and one of its new hand-drawn floats is seen here. The advert. for Grade "A" "TT" (Tuberculin Tested) milk is a reminder of the problems sometimes encountered with the smaller dairymen's facilities. Tuberculosis was a very real concern and milk was routinely delivered from the churn to open containers prior to the introduction of sterilised recyclable glass bottles with cardboard covers. (In 1925 Job's were advertising that their bottled milk was the same price as competitors' traditional offerings.)

ECHELFORD SCHOOL 1933

Photographed shortly after its opening in 1933, Echelford School was a revolutionary design from the County Architect's Department at a time of great financial stringency, when even teachers' salaries were being cut. Described as factory architecture adapted to school purposes, Ashford's futuristic new facility, only the second of its type, was echoed by Oakington Manor School, Wembley. The $2^1/_2$-acre site was originally built to accommodate 388 junior pupils in classrooms for up to 50. The whole edifice, with the adjacent caretaker's cottage, costing £12,500, was officially opened on 23rd December, 1933, by the Master of the Rolls, Lord Hanworth, its having been in use for a month before. Other features of the accommodation included indoor sanitary facilities and separate staff rooms for male and female teachers. The new school was still not of sufficient size to satisfy the ever-rising demand for places and by 1937 temporary wooden classrooms were erected at a cost of £655 plus £110 for furnishing them.

ECHELFORD SCHOOL, 1963

Large classes, by today's standards, were a continuing feature of the provision of state education – for instance, in commemoration of the Silver Jubilee of George V in 1935, 415 Echelford pupils were given medals confirming an average class size of over 50. The new facilities were soon caught up in the upheaval of the Second World War and such was the level of overcrowding that Echelford pupils were sharing the campus of the as yet unfinished Stanwell Road School with staff of the Army infantry records. Post-war education, at least for the juniors, settled down to a more regular routine and under the headships of Mr. Wilfred Morris and Mr. Thwaites, and aided by a dedicated staff, the school gained a strong reputation for music and drama. Seen here are pupils of Form 4A of 1963 with their teacher, Mr. Clarke. Front row left to right: Rhona Breakspeare, Hilary Munnings, Susan ?, Jennifer Read, Rosa Moore, Julia King, Susan Cliffe, ?, Sharon Winters, Linda Dixon. Second row: ?, Hazel Pire, Carol ?, Margaret Hughes, Francessca ?, ?, Marilyn Barker, Josephine Laslett, Patricia ?, Joyce Curry, Linda Wakefield. Third row: ?, ?, ?, Piers Chandler, ?, Christopher Minto, Kenneth ?, Peter Rudd, Robert Keen. Fourth row: ?, ?, David Constable, ?, ?, ?, ?, ?.

VOLUNTEER FIRE BRIGADE c. 1924

Ashford's Volunteer Fire Brigade, pictured here in their parade uniform, were possibly photographed on the occasion of the acquisition of their new machine based on that ubiquitous workhorse of the western world, a Ford Model "T" supplied by the Staines dealership, Crimbles. Costing £172 plus £19 for the Merryweather 20-foot double ladder, it had a top speed of 12 mph. Their previous machine, a horse-drawn steam pump acquired in 1907, was sold for £25. By 1932 the Ford was declared obsolete and the Ashford brigade acquired the "George the Fifth" engine from Staines in 1935. (see Snapshots of Staines, p. 21) The crew lived or worked nearby and were able to answer calls for their services in short order, summoned by a variety of means. On the right is the Brigade Captain, John H. Knight, caretaker of the County School, one of the founder members who had already served for nearly 20 years. Other volunteers at this time were Albert Wilson, groundsman of the County School, seated on the right; Mr. Albert Bailey, second from left, who worked at Spurr's Grocers, nearly opposite; Frank Barker, the Engineer; Mr. William Franklin and his son, Douglas; George Kimber from W.H. Smith's bookstall; Albert Belding; Harry Avis; and Harold Upton. A charge of £1 was made for attending fires in the parish and £6 outside. Neighbouring brigades would combine to cover major conflagrations outside the local area. The fire at the candle factory in Staines in 1924 is remembered by Mrs. Ward, the daughter of Mr. A. Wilson. When he returned home, his uniform was stiff with dried paraffin wax!

FIRE STATION, CHURCH ROAD, c. 1943

Ashford's fire brigade's depot, said to have been erected by Harry Richardson, opened in 1905. Large crowds gathered for the occasion: another demonstration that the area was rapidly changing from the old village with its main focus near the parish church to widespread settlement throughout the parish. As well as housing the brigade's equipment the building, as Parish and later Urban District Council property, also served a number of other purposes including that of mortuary (in an adjacent building) and as an office for Rate collection. On the tower can be seen the marker board recording the savings efforts of the town during Warship Week in March 1943. This national campaign was to encourage the whole population to subscribe, through savings bonds, towards the cost of the War effort and in particular warships. Ashford's target was set at £70,000, but at the end of the massive campaign a total of £91,472 had been pledged. The now demolished hose drying and practice tower was erected c. 1937 in anticipation of war and the need for comprehensive Civil Defence measures.

THE ROYAL HART HOTEL, CHURCH ROAD, 1911

Decorated all over for the Coronation of George V on 22nd June, 1911, the Royal Hart Hotel had already been serving refreshment to residents and visitors for at least 50 years. Its familiar signage depicted the favourite badge of King Richard II and represented a male red deer in its 5th year. By c. 1925, the façade as seen here had been rendered and given the fashionable mock timbered elevations, a bay window in the lounge bar and a glazed tiled plinth. The large ornate gas lamp over the door was originally a necessity at a time when public street lamps were non-existent in Ashford. In February 1912 the Ashford Lighting Committee approved the purchase of 13 second-hand columns and gas-lit lanterns from the corporation of the City of London for £13, the lights to be placed in strategic locations in the parish. Some public-spirited citizens paid for further lamps and it would seem that the one erected outside the Royal Hart was one of them! A reminiscence of Edwardian Ashford recalled Charlie's Fried Fish Stall outside the Royal Hart some time before 1910, mobile takeaways clearly having a long history.

THE ROYAL HART HOTEL, CHURCH ROAD, c. 1925

Much fascinating contemporary detail is contained in this pair of cards issued by the hotel, providing an excellent record of part of the interior of one of Ashford's licensed premises. The trade, ever keen to attract and keep clientele, were at this time facing even more competition for the custom of the general population. The plush cinemas springing up all over the country and the new phenomena of radio broadcasting and wider car ownership required new and better facilities; and a boom in re-building and re-vamping inns and public houses commenced in the mid-1920s. Local competition was also a factor, with new function facilities at the Hearts of Oak (see p. 57). One of the once-popular facilities at the Royal Hart was re-vamped in 1926 when the Landlord, Mr. F. Crowley, who had held the licence since 1903, announced that the billiard tables had been removed from the spacious hall adjoining the inn, which had been given over for special events. The Hart had also housed another indoor sport before the First World War when it hosted a skittle club and alley, "one of the finest in West Middlesex". The décor of the large room gave rise to the enduring appellation of "The Tudor Hall", which was soon hosting a wide range of live musical and other events.

CHURCH ROAD c. 1925

Sometimes identified as a clergyman, the gentleman about to mount his bike was in fact Dr. Benjamin Hague Dale, MRCS, LRCP, recalled as "much loved and greatly respected". His house on the far left, no. 25 Church Road, was also his surgery in the days when general practitioners routinely performed many operations in-house. Before the advent of the National Health Service in 1948, medical services were provided on a fee-paying basis for the majority of the population, with insurance and the local Nurse Fund for home visits and maternity care. In addition to the services of at least five physicians covering Ashford c. 1925, there were also maternity nurses at a time when the vast majority of births took place at home. Ashford's principal practitioner in the field was Nurse Mrs. Alice Rose of 41 Church Road. She had set up here in 1910 and by the time of her retirement in 1937 had attended the delivery of some 3,000 babies. Also available were private nursing homes. In 1926 Normanhurst, opposite St. Matthew's, advised that it treated medical, surgical and maternity cases, with fully trained staff and an up-to-date operating theatre.

WESTLAKE'S, 13 CHURCH ROAD, c. 1965

One of the earliest retail developments of the new town was "The Market Place" built by Frederick Field c. 1892. Part of this terrace, now no. 13 Church Road, has a long history of providing Ashfordians with a range of pharmaceutical and technical services. An early occupant, Walter Vincent Westlake, a dispensing chemist and druggist established here since 1910, was also involved in providing services to amateur photographers and in 1911 demonstrated "Autochromes" – a colour process introduced in 1907 – to the new Spelthorne Camera Club at Edward Nicholson's studio. Mr. Westlake also has a claim to fame as one of the earliest DJs. In October 1930 the Old Ashfordian Association held dances at the school, the music provided by his radio gramophone. In addition to selling records and radios and charging accumulators (a form of battery for those without mains electricity) he pioneered television receivers, demonstrating the system some years before the advent of the BBC in 1936. The two aspects of the business are seen here just after the premises were taken over in 1965 by fellow pharmacist Mr. E.W Breakspear, previously trading at 7 Station Parade since 1953.

CHURCH ROAD c. 1936

Along with the rise in Ashford's population there was a commensurate increase in retail outlets – in 1933 a survey reported that there were approximately 130 shops in Ashford. This view conveniently illustrates the changing face of architecture at the time with the traditional façade of the Market Place juxtaposed with the new parades combining shops with rented accommodation above. On the right, the new development offered shoppers a range of retailers including confectioners, grocers, butchers and greengrocers. The early 1930s – a period of national and worldwide economic depression – was conversely a boom time for new suburban housing and its associated facilities. Between 1932 and 1937 there had been 534 houses built within 1/2 mile radius of 70 Church Road. Responding to this situation, the Chairman of the newly-formed Ashford Chamber of Commerce was moved to comment on the competition between the Chamber and "that fester and sore of all trades, the price cutter, together with the chain bazaars and multiple stores which are no respecters of any business or trade."

JARMAN'S, 5 NEW PARADE c. 1938

A major new retail and residential development of the late 1930s was New Parade. Among the new tenants were both Tesco and Woolworth's, the type of enterprise then so loathed by the Chamber of Commerce, although other chain stores including Marks & Spencer and British Home Stores were specifically excluded by the terms of the leases offered. No. 5 New Parade was let to John Jarman on a 42-year lease at a rental of £225 per annum. Mr. Jarman was developing a chain of tobacconists and confectioners and eventually had premises in Addlestone, Ashford, Guildford, Walton-on-Thames, Weybridge and Wokingham. All his premises were recorded photographically, giving an evocative and invaluable record of a specialist retailer; and although many once well-loved brands and their products are lost, a number of today's familiar names introduced in the 1930s are still very popular, the contemporary point-of-sale advertising and retail prices seen here providing much interest and with loose sweets priced per quarter imperial lb. The scales on the tobacconist's counter are also a reminder that many varieties of pipe or hand rolling tobacco were originally sold loose by weight.

COUNTY LIBRARY, CHURCH ROAD c. 1975

Although newsagents and W.H. Smith maintained private circulating libraries stocking mainly novels, prior to the opening of the purpose-built County Library residents used branch libraries established in local authority schools. Originally housed at the Woodthorpe Road School in 1925, by 1937 there were 573 borrowers on the register at Clarendon Road, which opened on Monday and Saturday from 7.00 to 8.30 pm. The new County Library, its 14th branch, opened in Stanwell Road on 7th October, 1939. The facility, open 10.00 am to 7.00 pm, soon attracted a substantial clientele and during the first week 702 adults and 130 junior members were using the stock of 8,000 titles. A new centrally-located library was opened on Saturday, 12th January, 1963 following a service of dedication conducted by the Vicar of Ashford and over 10,000 books were issued during its first week. The new building included a dedicated children's room and hosted presentations by visiting celebrities, as seen here: in this case Tony Hart from the BBC television show "Vision On", the oak chairs in use being brought from the old library.

CHURCH ROAD AND CLARENDON ROAD, 10th AUGUST, 1929

An adjunct to the street scene postcards so readily available was the aerial view introduced post-World War I. The techniques refined over the battlefields were well utilised for commerce and the great value of such views can be seen here. The central area of open land, Cooks Field, was still used for the annual flower show. Much use was also beginning to be made of aerial photography for archaeological surveying. Unfortunately, the interesting-looking features seen in the Grammar School playing fields are almost certainly drainage or pitch markings. Fronting Church Road were some more of Ashford's lost trees, including elms and a magnificent oak removed when the Library was built in 1962. From the top of the tallest of these it was possible for children to observe the construction of the new Heathrow Central Tower and later Astronaut House near Feltham Station. Also observable here is the rapid suburbanisation of the area, with the layout of the road system and housing dictated by the pre-existing alignment of Church Road.

FLOWER SHOW c. 1910

Another symbol of the growth of the area was the Annual Show of the Ashford Horticultural and Industrial Society. From its inception in 1901 it was held on the conveniently central site of Cooks Field on the first Thursday afternoon in July – the then early closing day. The entries in the numerous classes were drawn from a complete cross-section of local society and also attracted support from a much wider area. A subject of numerous postcard views, the day's proceedings were much photographed. A newer technology, the movie camera, was also employed to record the happy scene. Although it is not clear whether the operator shown here with his hand-cranked camera was an amateur or a professional cameraman, the resulting reel of film would have had an appreciative audience. Local pioneer Cecil Hepworth of Walton-on-Thames (1874-1953) had been shooting short films since 1899: very few of these have survived, however, having fallen victim to the highly flammable nature of the film stock or been recycled for the silver content.

ASHFORD BRASS BAND c. 1905

At one time, towns large and small had their own bands and in many cases the non-conformist churches and temperance organisations also supported their own groups, with members often belonging to several bands. Ashford Brass Band is seen here at the newly established Horticultural and Industrial Show c. 1905, when the photograph indicates that they were able to muster 21 musicians. In February 1911 the Town Band had decided to give open-air concerts in various parts of the village during the evenings of the next two months with a view to raising funds for the purchase of new uniforms. Their Hon. Sec. was Mr. C. Parfitt of Park Road. A photograph depicting the band in 1911 shows 31 musicians and this enlarged corps headed processions in celebration of the coronation of George V on 22nd June. Following the outbreak of war and the volunteering and conscription of musicians, the band seems to have ceased playing, although post-war, the newly-formed British Legion branch formed its own band and boys of the District School continued to play for special events in the area.

COUNTY SCHOOL c. 1925

Pupils of the County School are shown learning shorthand and touch-typing. This was one of a series of six cards issued by the school showing the range of facilities available. Others show the gymnasium, laboratory, domestic science rooms, etc. A rise in the annual fees to £15 5s in 1922 seems to have led to a decline in the numbers on the roll and a subsequent reduction to £3 3s a term. The machines in use for the lessons were probably the ubiquitous American Underwood no. 5 dating from 1900. More than three million of the model were produced and sold worldwide and would have cost the education authority around £12 each at a time when the average weekly wage for a male clerk was around £4 10s. One of the masters at the County School also took a very practical interest in the technology of the typewriter when in 1926 Mr. W.H. Jones entered a patent no. 246015 for an improved machine. Its chief advantage consisted of one lever instead of numerous ones, which it was hoped would reduce much of the irritating clatter. Mr. Jones was reportedly helped in this by one of the pupils, Clifford Elliot.

CHURCH ROAD c. 1950

Ashford Grammar School's imposing entrance, surmounted by the arms of Middlesex County Council, was the traditional focus for recording school groups. On the first day of the first term of the new school there were 46 pupils on the roll, rising to 94 by the beginning of the following term. A whole school group of that year shows 80 scholars and 5 teaching staff under the headship of Mr. J.W.B. Adams, with the 32 girls wearing uniform and straw boaters and the boys in uniform and caps. Photographic evidence also shows that within ten years of its completion the façade was completely covered in its familiar cladding of Virginia creeper. Pictured here are form 4F of 1949/50. Back row, left to right: Raymond Atkins, Rodney Gabriel, Neville Gunn, Jean Whitby, Ann Lodge, Mary Marsh, Gill Henderson, Yvonne Pilbeam, Josephine Cooper, ?, Aubrey Appleton, Phillip Hazel, P. Hayman. Second Row: Jill Everard, Jill Harris, ?, ?, ?, Mr. M. Davey (Science and Physics Master), Vivienne Plum, Jean Phillips, Wendy Wright, Anna O' Reilly, Ann Claxton. Bottom Row: B. Quelch, ?, ?, ? Williams ?, Peter Dawson.

THE POST OFFICE, CHURCH ROAD, 1924 & 1964

Ashford's purpose-built post office and telephone exchange had been open for 16 years when this view was taken in 1924. The village's original receiving house for the collection and despatch of mail was part of Mr. Bennett's bakery and grocer's shop in Feltham Hill Road, later occupied by Bayley's. Members of the Bennett family were involved in this important service from at least 1845, Miss Rosa Bennett taking charge of the enhanced service available from here in 1908. At this time telephone services in the area were provided not only by the Post Office but also the National Telephone Company, originally formed in 1881, who had their call office in Clarendon Road by 1910. Apart from a few municipal services the Post Office became a monopoly in 1912, a local directory of 1915 suggesting that Ashford had c. 50 private and commercial subscribers. The public call box was of a type soon to be succeeded by the new KI design introduced in 1921, which replaced the wooden kiosks of varying design then in use. Further changes to the national telecommunications system were taking place at this time. In 1922 the Post Office was experimenting with the "Strowger" system for automatic telephone exchanges which were in national use by 1924, although the Ashford exchange did not become fully automatic until 1964. Over 4,300 local phones were converted to Subscriber Trunk Dialling on the 5th March, the process accomplished by the team of volunteer engineers seen here. Ashford's postal history has been the subject of a comprehensive study by Graham Smeed, published to celebrate the 50th anniversary of the Ashford Philatelic Society in 2003.

CHURCH ROAD c.1936

Ashford's prominent war memorial angel now surveys an environment very different from its original surroundings when first placed here in 1921. Some of the green fields it then faced had by now recently been built on with the new shops, typical of the inter-war developments, which were designed to be lit by electricity and took advantage of the latest building techniques, including the use of mass-produced metal windows etc. Seen here are the premises of the Holly Cash Stores and ironmongers Mountfield. "Studholme", the adjacent surgery of Dr. John Scott, seems to be the new site of the commemorative gas lamp erected in 1911, which once occupied the memorial island. Decorative ironwork fencing around the flowerbeds added in 1923 was the work of Clarendon Road plumber Albert Chase. By 1926 the memorial required thorough renovation involving dressing the stonework, repainting the names and inscription and repainting the enclosing railings with aluminium paint. The detached memorial to the fallen of the Second World War was first mooted in 1951 to cost c.£136 and unveiled in 1953, once again funded by public subscription.

ROYAL AIR FORCE ASSOCIATION ASHFORD HEADQUARTERS (THE ALBATROSS CLUB), CHURCH ROAD, c. 1951

Ashford's branch of the Royal Air Force Association was formed in 1949 with around 30 members and by July 1951 were ready to open the Albatross Club in premises at 77 Church Road. The building, previously a rented private house, was typical of the large late-Victorian houses which once fronted this part of Church Road. Work to prepare the building for its new use was carried out by the members, including conversion from gas to electric lighting, fitting out the building with a lounge, billiard and darts rooms, a bar and landscaping the grounds. Membership was open to serving members of the R.A.F. and W.R.A.F. and also ex-members of the R.F.C., R.N.A.S., Auxiliary Air Force and other associated bodies. The opening ceremony was performed by Air Marshall Sir Robert Soundby, KBE, CBM, DFC, AFC. Branch membership drawn from Ashford, Staines, Stanwell, Laleham, Shepperton and Sunbury was also heavily involved in the annual Battle of Britain parade held every September: by the late 1950s, however, the Club was reported as being not well used and was advertised for private hire.

ASTORIA, CHURCH ROAD, 1939 & 1975

The licensing authority, the Middlesex County Council, provisionally approved plans for a new cinema in Ashford in February 1935. The site was to be in Church Road, one report suggesting that its location was to have been that now occupied by the Ashford Library; and it was to be called The Regal. In the event The Astoria, originally the name of a select area of Long Island, New York, named after Jacob Astor, was opened on Monday, 30th October, 1939. Members of the Perrin family were the proprietors and had been running a cinema in Clarendon Road (see p.31). The new 1,200-seat venue, replete with all the latest technical innovations and plush upholstered seating, opened for business just after the commencement of the Second World War. This event no doubt coloured the sentiments of the owners, who advised new patrons that: "The Astoria was built by British people of British materials including the organ and talkie apparatus. The staff were chosen from the area and work under British supervision." Hold- ups and delays in its completion were also noted. Shortage of materials and expert labour at this time are well remembered: one Ashford Master Builder recalled a sudden respect for tradesmen by Ashfordians who wanted brick air raid shelters built!

One feature of the cinema was the introduction of a Compton three-manual Theatrone organ as seen here being played by Edgar Peto, previously at the Hounslow Cinema and well known on the London cinema circuit. This instrument was truly a British and indeed a local product; the Compton Company of Acton developing Clifford Road resident Mr. L.E.A. Bourn's electrostatic tone generation technology into the highly successful pipeless organs. The first film shown here was "A Girl Must Live" with Margaret Lockwood: the last picture show on 13th December,1975, featured Gene Wilder in "Young Frankenstein". Subsequently run as a Bingo Club by Mecca Leisure Ltd., this in turn closed in 1998, the housing complex erected being given the name of the original developers of the site.

CHURCH ROAD, 10th August, 1928.

The antiquity of the Parish Church and its graveyard meant that by 1910, even with an additional plot added in 1895, the area available for interments was reaching capacity. The situation was relieved in that year by the opening of a new Council-run cemetery in the London Road, the first interment there, that of a sister from the Convent, taking place on April 21st. The churchyard also dictated the road alignment here and the consequent narrowing was relieved in 1963 by reducing the frontages of the premises opposite. Of all the large detached residences seen here, only the vicarage, built in 1876, remains. The largest of these, "Normanhurst", had a chequered history after its use as nursing home (see p. 39) and by 1930 the house and grounds were being suggested as a site for a factory. The open land opposite the "Parade" on the corner of Percy Road, a plot 48 feet by 169 feet, was soon to be considered as a site for a Parish Hall: a proposal in 1930 by the London Diocesan Fund to purchase the site was approved by the new Staines Urban District Council.

94 CHURCH ROAD c. 1935

Following the long-established tradition of photographically recording the start of a new venture, we see here Mr. Herbert Utting and staff posing outside his new shop at 94 Church Road. Another grocer, Frank White, had previously operated the premises, part of the "Parade" on Church Road. Mr. Utting, a Fellow of the Grocers' Institute, also had a connection with a similar business at St. John's Wood, London, and had won a gold medal for his tea and coffee at a trade exhibition in 1911. In addition to the contemporary displays of groceries, we see evidence of the environmentally friendly delivery system offered by many retailers at that time and much later. Also seen is the cycle rack then provided outside many shops as a service to customers. Apart from brands still familiar as products of multi-national food companies, such stores supplied a wide range of other tinned and dried goods at a time when most breadwinners were paid weekly and frozen food was limited to ice cream. Mr. Utting typically also offered weekly credit to his regular clientele.

THE PARADE c. 1950

Prior to the advent of "The Parade" c. 1903, Ashford's parish church stood isolated on the north side of Church Road. The new shopping facility of seven retailers was provided with a marked advantage over the other new premises springing up in the village. Seven gas-lit street lamps along the pavement plus the individual shops' own illumination gave Ashfordians shopping here the chance to view the goods in the evening. Although gas supplies from the Egham Causeway plant were available from 1891, these ostentatious street lamps were the only public lighting in the area at this time. Late night opening was the norm, with retailers of all types often open until 10.00 p.m. or later on Friday and Saturday to coincide with the then usual paydays. Half-day closing for Ashford's shop assistants was originally set for Thursdays but had changed to the more familiar Wednesday by 1914. By 1950 the seven varied traders here were Messrs. Whittington, Holland & Barratt, Morgan, Galliford, Stevenson, The Southern Wool Co, and Fullers.

ST. MATTHEW'S / ST. MICHAEL'S c. 1910

St. Matthew's possesses two bells pre-dating the present church and its immediate predecessor. These were cast by a local specialist: the Eldridge bell foundry of Chertsey, members of whose family were working in the town between 1619 and 1716. A third bell was cast by Meares & Stainbank of Whitechapel in 1797, presumably in connection with the new church completed in the same year, and was re-cast by them in 1914. Two further bells added in 1980 and 1981 were also cast in London. At the end of the 19th century these Anglican bells had a modest rival in those used by the nearby convent for their own services. These were the subject of an action at law in 1903-4 because of the reputed annoyance caused by their ringing. Another local campanological connection is still to be found in the survival of the re-erected clock tower at the Clockhouse Lane Recreation Ground. Here, the bell accompanying the clock mechanism is said to date to the mid 18th century. Plans for another set of bells in the area did not materialise. Original designs for St. Hilda's included a tower and spire and the Will of the Reverend Thornton, published following his death in 1930, called for a peal of least eight bells here.

ST. MATTHEW'S CHOIR OUTING c. 1910

The Parish's long-established choral tradition meant that by 1909 the church maintained an all-male choir under long-standing Organist and Choirmaster Thomas Pace, consisting of 15 trebles, 4 altos, 5 tenors and 6 basses. Also in keeping with tradition, the body had a social aspect, with outings part of the regular calendar and horse-drawn trips to Box Hill and London Theatres reported. Other local churches maintained similar bodies whose choristers also enjoyed annual outings. In 1912, for example, Ashford's Wesleyan Methodist choir and up to 200 supporters enjoyed a river trip to Taplow aboard the "La Marguerite", departing from the Town Hall steps, Staines. The Thames was the focus of a booming tourist trade, with pleasure craft large and small to the fore. Other beneficiaries of this trade were the professional photographers. At the various locks en route they would record the day-trippers and supply prints on the return journey, a convivial journey and appropriate refreshment, as seen in the stern, adding to the enjoyment of the outing at a time when many of the adult population routinely worked six days a week.

THE TOWN TREE c. 1930

By the time of its demise in 1952, Ashford's "Town Tree" (an elm) was estimated to be approximately 175 years old. The name's derivation has led to much speculation – was the appellation "Town" an indication of Georgian aggrandisement or some hint that the area had archaeological features suggestive of substantial occupation? Parish records of 1776 note either this tree as a sapling, or its predecessor, as the site of the village stocks – a convenient central location to exhibit delinquent villagers. When the stocks were removed is not clear, but the site subsequently became home to the distinctive granite feature seen here. This combined trough and drinking fountain was one of the network of watering points erected by the Metropolitan Drinking Fountain & Cattle Trough Association, founded in 1859 to provide clean water to animals and humans. By 1900, thousands had been erected under the auspices of the association and individual charity, Ashford's example being sponsored by Mrs. Seppings of Chattern House, the widow of a former Vicar of Ashford, in 1902. The trough and a replacement tree, an oak, have been moved to nearby locations.

EXEFORD AVENUE. ASHFORD. JWM. 6633

EXEFORD AVENUE c. 1930

Another of Ashford's new street names which recognised historic origins, Exeford Avenue was a post-First World War development. Although the line of Exeford Avenue had been laid out by c. 1913, it appears that construction did not start until after the end of the war. A report of 1920 described the new houses as containing four bedrooms, two living rooms, kitchen, scullery and bathroom and constructed with "Australian Concrete Blocks". It is not clear if this account refers to the importation of materials or a patented system in use in the UK. In 1930, residents complained about the condition of the road but did acquire their first street lamp and, along with many other residential roads, the Avenue was included in the 1935 scheme to make up many of Ashford's roads at a cost of £9,560. The photograph bears the imprint of Joseph Warren Mortimer of "Woodbine", Wolsey Road – at the same address as that of William Applebee's concern. This, and the continuation of the Applebee numbering sequence, may suggest that Mr. Mortimer was professionally associated with the company and took it over for a short time.

PARKLAND GROVE c. 1913

"X" marks the home of the sender of this view, posted in August 1921, although the original date of the exposure is sometime before the summer of 1914. The property, "Ludlow", may have been one of the many houses in the street built by Henry Richardson of Feltham Road. However, the building of the estate from the late 1890s caused the ditch which originally drained the land to become blocked. In 1921 the path was said to be in a "terrible" state. A correspondent to the Middlesex Chronicle was of the opinion that this was the chief road of Ashford and it was high time it was made up properly! The tree planting which possibly gave the "Grove" its appellation seems to have been a mixed blessing, as another correspondent in 1929 was concerned that the street lights here were "artfully concealed between the trees so that Ashfordians should not notice whether they were lighted or not." By 1935 the local authority undertook to make up that part of the road not already resurfaced as part of the comprehensive scheme for many of Ashford's thoroughfares.

Parkland Grove, Ashford.   W.H.A. 1897

CLOCKHOUSE LANE RAILWAY BRIDGE c. 1914

The coming of the railway in 1848 radically altered Clockhouse Lane, the ancient link between the London Road and Ashford village. Indeed this bridge and others constructed for it are now some of the area's oldest structures! The position of the new feature directly on the boundary between two parishes, and later two local authorities, seems to have caused dispute between the bodies as to its upkeep. In 1905, Staines and Feltham Councils were querying the agreement drawn up in 1899 between them and the London & South Western Railway Company as to who was responsible for bridge maintenance. The Lane itself had also been a subject of interest to local planners for many years. In 1925 a proposal was reported which would have completely altered its character. The Great West Road was to run down Clockhouse Lane to the pond and then through the Convent grounds to the top of School Lane, joining the Chertsey Bypass. Residents also had to contend with another problem: in September 1929 attention was drawn to the necessity for a proper footpath here when water ran off the road into an adjoining property and swamped the kitchen!

REEDSFIELD ROAD 1913

Another Applebee production illustrates what was then a relatively new development. Ten years later a local councillor raised the possibility of a street light here, only to be advised that part of the road was in Feltham Council's area. Reedsfield Road's main claim to fame is its eponymous residents' association, started after the 1945 peace celebrations. It was said that during the War, Reedsfield Road had raised more for the War effort than any other road in Ashford. This communal spirit was manifest in their own street celebration; and the Residents' Association of about 70 members which covered the road and the northern end of Clockhouse Lane started their meeting in the nearby St. Michael's Hall. Within eight years the group had its own hall open in time for the Coronation of Elizabeth II in 1953. This building, erected on blitzed land, had an interesting history, reputedly being built originally for the Wembley Exhibition in 1922/23. Subsequently used by the Boys' Brigade in Staines, it was re-erected and fitted out by the efforts of the Association.

THE CLOCK HOUSE c. 1929/30

A photographic record of the origin of the road name illustrates the mansion house and stable block surmounted by the eponymous horological feature. The building had features suggestive of an early 18th-century date and with its ancillary buildings was the focus of many postcard views. One report suggests that the grounds had contained an icehouse – an underground feature that allowed perishable food to be stored before refrigeration. Was this structure the origin of rumours of Roman remains in the area? By August 1935, in spite of approaches to the National Trust and other bodies, the house was being demolished: its clock tower was offered to the Council and incorporated into the octagonal shelter of the new recreation ground. The pond in the foreground, another of Ashford's lost water features, was both picturesque and dangerous. In January 1926 local hero Leslie Serpant saved two boys from drowning in its six feet of water, they having fallen through the ice. In 1930, plans to convert it into a paddling pool for the proposed recreation ground were dropped on the grounds of cost.

CLOCK HOUSE LANE, 1937

Following the loss of "The Clock House" in 1935/6, the land was utilised for a small estate by the Eltham firm of Lincoln & Darby. Advertised as "Darby"-built houses, the contemporary publicity advises prospective purchasers of its unique position overlooking the recreation ground with its tennis courts, rugby and association football grounds and beautifully-kept flower beds and playgrounds for children, "making life worth living for young and old!" The developers also somewhat optimistically suggested that the new homes were eight minutes from Ashford Station. These "soundly constructed" houses, equipped with all modern labour-saving devices, cost from £515 freehold. However, the condition of the street itself was of concern at the same time and the local authority was asking Middlesex County Council to take steps to widen it. The original "kink" in the thoroughfare so clearly visible here was straightened out soon afterwards. Further along, at the junction of Parkland Road and Clockhouse Lane, a projecting hedge at Archers Lodge was also adjusted at a cost of £29 9s 10d, all helping to improve the standard of the lane.

STITTS COTTAGE c. 1936

Photographs indicate that Stitts Cottage, previously Clock House Farm, was a remarkable survival of a late medieval building. A 1939 Middlesex County Council survey suggests a probable 17th century date, much altered but with two original windows; however, external features such as the central chimneystack and timber framing suggest a converted open hall house with a central hearth, possibly of 15th century date. Graham Smeed observed wattle and daub features in the structure, another indication of its early date. Appropriately, the eponymous occupier in 1926, printer John Muir Stitt, proposed to publish "Old Ashford Records". This was to be an illustrated record of the parish from the earliest time and would contain previously unpublished material. Local support was not encouraging and the following announcement was published in The Middlesex Chronicle: "Owing to the magnificent response made by the parishioners, 97 out of the required minimum 800 (print run) Old Ashford Records will not be published". It is not known what material he intended to include: however, the "Ashford Year Book and Blotter" published the same year by Stitts contains much local historical information.

STITTS COTTAGE c. 1936

John Muir Stitt and son came to Ashford c. 1919 and commenced a printing and publishing business from here. One of their earliest imprints was the "Clock House Press" and, as "Southcottians" (followers of the 19th-century mystic Joanna Southcott), they printed all the organisation's material. Stitt was also for many years the printer of St. Matthew's Parish Magazine and a myriad other local documents. As seen here, there were other sidelines emanating from the cottage, and as well as apples from the orchard, the firm were recorded as paper bag suppliers and in 1949, bookbinding was a speciality. John Stitt was clearly interested in local history and in 1951 was recorded as owning a plan of Ashford dated 1760 and having found several coins of late 16th and early 17th century date in one of the cottage's ceilings before the war. By 1956 Stitts Cottage was sold for development and the possibly medieval building demolished. A postcard of Stitts Cottage showing the rear elevation and many other local publications are available from Spelthorne Museum, Staines Library. Open Wednesday and Friday 2-4pm, Saturday 1-4pm.

ST. MICHAEL'S CHURCH c. 1914

Ashford's Roman Catholic community originally worshipped at a church dedicated to St. Michael, erected in 1906 on the site of the old parish gravel pit. The Archbishop of Westminster opened the work of local builder Arthur Francis, of Station Road, on 23rd December, 1906. As well as Ashford, the new building also served Catholics in East and West Bedfont, Littleton and Stanwell. Following the opening of the new church in Fordbridge Road, the original premises became the Catholic parish's church hall. By 1940 it was in use as St. John's School, with the occupier recorded as Mr. C. Grimsdale. However, later in the same year the building was listed as the "Coolbeg Private School". This was described as a day school for boys and girls, Principal, Miss R. Dallaston. The appellation "Coolbeg" is interesting, representing a place name in the Irish Republic adjacent to another settlement called Ashford in County Wicklow. In 1968 the old church was sold and subsequently demolished, a new hall and presbytery having been constructed on the Fordbridge Road site.

FELTHAM ROAD/CLOCK HOUSE LANE POND c. 1924

Prior to the introduction of standardised street signs, local direction signage was the responsibility of the relevant local authority. The 1903 Motor Car Act provided legislation for standardised warning and speed limit signs. By 1921, in response to the enormous increase in road traffic and speed, a Government circular to local authorities suggested extending this to the earlier system. However, the "finger post" seen here is typical of the wooden indicators more easily read by an earlier generation of slow-moving horse-drawn, bicycle and pedestrian traffic. The view also provides another record of the Parish Pond. In July 1912 Councillors were suggesting either filling in or cleansing it and in March 1921 there were further complaints about its foul condition, with Parish Councillors voicing the opinion that the only way to prevent the nuisance was to fill it with clean material. This was said to be out of the question as it would cost too much, and it was stated that liability lay with its owner, the Lord of the Manor.

CLOCK HOUSE CORNER c. 1930

This striking image illustrates one of the many changes in local topography within living memory, the unknown photographer of this beautifully composed view of Clock House Corner capturing yet another of Ashford's lost vistas. Even the local authority, concerned at a request to cut or trim the trees in the lane in 1921, reported there being no obstruction and that cutting the trees would destroy one of the few beautiful spots in Ashford! The water feature strategically situated at the junction of Clockhouse Lane and Feltham Road served many varied uses as the Parish Pond until it was filled in c. 1933. The brick arch seen on the left was the end of the old culvert draining the Parkland Grove area (see p. 50). A similar view sent to an address in Doncaster in May 1931 records that the sender was "having a marvellous time (in Ashford and had) been to Brooklands. Saw some topping cars, danced quite a good deal and seen some good shows."

THE KING'S HEAD, 1959

Apart from the Established Church, licensed premises are among the oldest institutions in many communities. Ashford's King's Head, in its central position, may be assumed to have an extremely long history, although its true age and the monarch originally commemorated in its sign are open to conjecture. Typically used as a meeting place for transacting parochial business, it was used by St. Michael's vestry in 1796 when arranging the building of the new parish church. Another contemporary establishment, the Queen's Head, first mentioned in 1767 – its location in the village unknown - may have been an alternative name for the same house. Following the 1830 Beer Act, any rate-paying householder could retail beer, ale and cider without a licence. Thousands of these "beerhouses" sprang up and in 1837 Ashford also boasted "The Green Man" and "The Traveller's Friend". The King's Head survived, at one time with an extensive collection of stabling, pigsties and a coach house. Its owners were the Isleworth Brewery, who had plans to redevelop the house before the Second World War and again in 1958 when appealing against the opening of the "AshTree".

FELTHAM ROAD c. 1933

The Chattern Hill Post Office at 39 Feltham Road opened in 1931 and served the local community until its closure on 29th September, 1999. In 1933 John Cooksey was listed as "confectioner and post office" at this address and the sign outside his shop advertises the family's other business: J. Cooksey & Son, electricians, plumbers and heating engineers, opposite at no. 42. The firm were established in 1883 and listed as smiths. In 1922 they also operated as house furnishers from the Market Place in Church Road. Seen here in front of the shop is a K3 type phone box. This type was designed by Sir Giles Gilbert Scott, architect of St. Michael's, Fordbridge Road, and constructed of reinforced concrete, costing half the price of the cast iron K2 type. Introduced in 1927, they were painted cream, which was considered to be in keeping with rural settings. Some 12,000 were installed throughout the country but proved fragile due to the materials used. Readers are also advised to consult the magisterial study of the area, by R. Calder, "A Place called Chattern Hill" (Gables Publishing 2003).

HEARTS OF OAK, FELTHAM ROAD, c. 1919

Many licensed premises had an "outreach programme" and regular deliveries of recyclable bottled beers and other bulk items were made by various means of transport. Pictured outside the Royal Hart, Stanley Richardson's Hearts of Oak turnout drawn by "Neddie" was typical of many local enterprises and won second prize in the Ashford Tradesmen's Competition held in conjunction with the Horticultural Show c. 1919. The Hearts of Oak played a central rôle in the social life of the area and supported a wide range of organisations. Meetings of some of these were held in the old Club Room, which pre-dated Stanley Hall, the new function room built c. 1925 and named after the landlord. Its famous outdoor quoits team founded c. 1897 was still playing in 1930 and meetings of the newly-formed Royal Order of Antediluvian Buffaloes (Echelford Lodge), the Exeford Masonic Lodge, the Harmonic Society and a branch of the recently-created British Legion meant that the premises were well patronised. A "slate club" formed c. 1885 to hold small regular savings for Christmas and members' welfare, and the largest of the Ashford clubs, was also based here.

LABURNHAM COTTAGE, FELTHAM ROAD, c. 1933

The retail premises at no. 97 Feltham Road were originally a private residence, Laburnham Lodge, a four-bedroomed house with stabling and outbuildings erected c. 1851. After the First World War, owner Mr. O'Shea converted it to a shop. By 1933 it was being run as The Laburnum Laundry and newsagents and general store by Mrs. Edith Silver and in 1937 by F.L. and R.T. McBride, whose family remained here until 2000. The present façade, although much altered and extended following war-time damage, is still home to one of Ashford's most intriguing inhabitants. "Little Sam", a copy of the original "Portland" cement statue has sat in his niche here since the mid 1800s. This representation of the biblical prophet Samuel was thought to be one of a number of casts produced by James Aspdin, son of the originator of the waterproof cement first patented by Joseph Aspdin of Leeds in 1824. One of the first occupiers of the original cottage was Stephen King, an architect who mortgaged the property in 1854. His profession allowed him access to architectural features, and perhaps young Samuel was a flourish of his.

FELTHAM ROAD c. 1923

As well as showing a traffic-free road, it is possible that the Applebee Company's photographer has also recorded for posterity a fascinating aspect of the local geology. The two large stone masses on the left-hand verge may be examples of either "sarsen stone", a type of sandstone found in the local ground and gravel as erratic boulders and also familiar from its use at Stonehenge, or pieces of iron and gravel conglomerate known as "ironstone". Around 1900, A.W. Smith, the Feltham horticultural entrepreneur, noted this particular substance, still found in parts of eastern Ashford in his new orchard (see p.61). Here, some very large masses of the concretion had to be cleared with dynamite prior to being steam ploughed to a depth of two feet. Locally, much deeper diggings for the new water reservoirs may also have been a source. Examples of both materials can be seen in a number of mediaeval buildings; and particularly churches – St. Lawrence, Chobham, being a spectacular example.

FELTHAM ROAD, 3rd June, 1932

Following the opening of the 230-acre London Air Park at Hanworth in 1929, local residents were soon familiar with a variety of aircraft using the site. Airport facilities on the borders of Ashford have a long history, however, and if a proposal of 1910 had come to pass the subsequent development of the area would have been very different. In January of that year Louis Blériot was preparing to build an "Aviation Centre" at Staines Moor "which would properly become the greatest centre of aviation in England"! Like Blériot's own machines (see p.13), the slow-moving Graf Zeppelin airship was a natural subject for contemporary photographers visiting Hanworth in 1931 and 1932. The image also neatly captured for posterity the new developments of local builders Sandell & Wren, the eponymous originators of Wren's and Sandell's Avenues in 1929. Herbert Sandell & Co. of 53 Wren's Avenue also advertised another sideline in 1930 – "Coal & Coke Merchant, General Haulage and Private Cars of all descriptions for hire day or night".

R.E.M.E DEPOT, FELTHAM ROAD, 1947

Ashford's R.E.M.E (Royal Electrical & Mechanical Engineers) workshop was established in September 1943 when some land in Feltham Road was taken over under the Defence of the Realm Act. R.E.M.E itself was formed on 10th October, 1942, to rationalise the repair facilities of the British Army. Military staffing consisted of three companies of R.E.M.E personnel, the complex being designated 1 Central Workshop. In 1953 the workshop was re-designated 31 Base Workshop and, following a general rationalization of facilities, closed progressively during 1957. This closure and the redundancies for the 500-strong civilian workforce led to many protests. The site, the only one in the U.K. to work on non-fighting vehicles, was said to have had the capacity to manufacture any given item, including special vehicle bodies, sheet metal components and foundry capacity. Typically, photography at military bases was generally not permitted and so far no other images of the complex are known – however, this "official" photograph shows that the Army personnel were able to erect and enjoy their very own pub, "Ye Craftsman's Arms".

POPLAR ROAD c. 1900

One of the most interesting residential developments in Ashford was the construction of the original Poplar Road Estate, named after the model farm and bungalow farmhouse. Given the soubriquet "Tin Town", up to 18 corrugated iron bungalows were built in Poplar and Coolgardie Roads and seem to have been connected with the local firm of T.J. Hawkins & Co., who were listed as horticultural builders in 1899 and previously as nurserymen and florists. Another Ashford firm, Ernest Hawkins, are also variously listed as horticultural builders and iron building contractors. By 1909 the company seems to have been operating on a very large scale, with premises in London and Liverpool, and were the builders of the new Woodthorpe Road School (see p. 11). They were also involved in other high-value projects including a contract with the Italian Government to supply 1,250 iron huts for the survivors of the catastrophic Messina earthquake of December 1908. As well as erecting many of the buildings for the Franco-British Exhibition held at the

White City in 1908, the firm also built two sets of barracks for the British Army at Frimley, Surrey. Although a number were demolished or damaged during the war, the last of these homes survived until 1992, a testimonial to the quality of the design and workmanship. The photograph shows Elizabeth Palmer and two sons, William and Charles.

ASHFORD AIRCRAFT WORKS c. 1918

One of the largest ever influxes of refugees occurred during the early days of the First World War when up to 250,000 Belgians arrived in the United Kingdom. Ashford, along with communities around the country, welcomed these victims of German aggression and many were integrated into War Work against the common enemy. It is not clear how many of the personnel seen here were locals and how many refugees it is, however, known that they were engaged in the production of wooden components for aircraft, including wings, at a site at Hawkins' Yard near the junction of Feltham Hill Road and Poplar Road. It is reported that, after the War, the works were taken over by the UK concessionaries of Citroen Cars, whose Type "A" open tourer went into production in May 1919 following a massive advertising campaign. The cars were imported from the Paris factory to Ashford and serviced here by Messrs. Gaston Ltd. prior to delivery to agents around the country. By March 1925 the works were disused when a fire destroyed offices and other buildings on the site.

SKITTRALL'S ENGINE c. 1890

A dramatic illustration of Ashford's role in what was once a rich arable landscape is the photograph of William Skittrall's traction engine and accompanying threshing machine. Mr. Skittrall's family, originally natives of Burbage, Wiltshire, had moved to Hersham, Surrey, by 1871 and Ashford by 1881. The makers, Wallis & Stevens of Basingstoke, sold the 10 hp engine new to the partnership of Clayton & Skitrall in June 1875. Described variously as a threshing machine owner and intriguingly in 1890 as a traction engine manufacturer, the 1881 census gives some indication of the size of Skittrall's enterprise, with William described as a worker of a threshing machine, employing eleven men, with three of his sons also working. Steam power, which had revolutionised travel by land and sea, had been harnessed for agricultural purposes, leading to the establishment of specialised contractors who could plough both deeper and faster than horse teams and process the resulting crops. Based at "Mayfield", Feltham Hill Road, Skittrall's also possessed two 7 hp traction engines bought new from Wallis & Stevens in 1899 and 1910 and both later sold to F. & A. Merick of Laleham. In keeping with the general road traffic at the time, the speed of these peripatetic power plants was generally not a problem: however, an incident of 1910 illustrates a familiar situation. One of the firm's engines, while proceeding along Feltham Hill Road in October 1910, broke an axle opposite "Tankerville", holding up traffic for the rest of the day.

FELTHAM HILL ROAD, 1928

Further indication of the local agricultural landscape still to be seen within living memory is illustrated here. In the far distance, to the left of the straight alignment of Feltham Hill Road, can be seen the serried rows of fruit trees, part of the 70-acre orchard planted by Feltham's A.W. Smith around 1900 (see p.58). The story of his remarkable enterprise is told in "The Great A.W. Smith" compiled and edited by R. Calder (2000). The road itself was soon to see some major upheavals, with the 1929 scheme to increase the width from 40 to 50 feet, the laying of main drainage starting in 1933 and the takeover of the maintenance of School Road by the County Council. The grounds of the Ecclesfield estate with its distinctive pond and central island were still farmed, one memory describing the fields covered in a mass of poppies during summer. Residential developments were soon to alter the scene, but some long-standing problems for pedestrians were still to be addressed by the County Council.in 1930. By 1943 there were further complaints about the lack of a footpath between Poplar Road and the Sunbury border, whilst a margin 10 feet wide in front of the houses was lower than the roadway, causing a quagmire in winter!

SCHOOL ROAD, 1959

Ashford's Church of England School has some claim to being the second oldest publ. institution in the area. Its foundation in 181. was due to the subscriptions of a number of local gentlemen and ladies who advanced capital to purchase government annuities, the income being used to support the Sunda. School Charity. By 1867 a building leased by the charity and described as a "temporar. wooden structure" was in use for the school. This was replaced the next year by a new brick building erected in what was originall. Denton Road and re-named School Road. The building consisted of a three-bedroome. house for the head teacher and four classrooms. Additional accommodation was erected in 1878 and 1883. Substantial improvements carried out in 1933 included the provision of three new classrooms, a playing field, a new water supply and replacement of the antiquated sanitary system. Also introduced in this year was the "Old Nationals' Association", the forerunne. of the present parent/teacher association. Further major improvements were started i. 1959, when Church Road photographer Bill. Dray pictured the procession of St. Matthew's choir and pupils at the dedication of the foundation stone of the new assembl. hall by the Bishop of Kensington on February 28th.

SCHOOL ROAD, 1963

Pictured here are Class 5 of 1963. Top row left to right: Kevin Jones, Richard Beeston, Martin Cooper, Stephen Allen, John Lenz, Ian Farmer, Colin Cornish, Christopher Thompson, David Wheeler, Dakin Crane. Second row: Gary Spooner, Linda Carpenter, Yvonne Mountjoy, Rowena Marshall, Janet Burridge, Gillian Woods, Gloria Milton, Deborah Taylor, Karen Burridge, Pauline Rodgers, Lesley Purvis, Paul Strutt. Bottom row: Jane Tugwell, Angela Shaw, Kathleen Harbourne, Debbie Henwood, Janet Lee, Lorraine Williams, Susan Dunn, Linda Ward, Julie Rawson. The Form Teacher was Mrs. Housam. Their Headteacher, Mr. F.G. Stickler, was Head from 1954 to 1974 and introduced the House System named after four of the school's benefactors, heads or managers. Further developments took place in 1965 when the block forming the present Middle School was erected.

ROWLAND HILL AND VAUGHAN ALMSHOUSES c. 1907

Another institution removed to rural Ashford in the 19th century was the charitable foundation originally set up near London's Blackfriars Road in 1811. Following the laying of the foundation stone on 12th July, 1894, the new facility on a one-and-a-half-acre site was opened on 19th March, 1895. A later report gives some idea of the contrasting environs for the inhabitants: "The sisters have three rooms instead of one, pure country air in place of South London fog and smoke, the song of the birds in place of the cry of the costermongers and the scream of the neighbouring railway engines, the sweet scent of the surrounding fields instead of the odours from the adjacent slaughterhouses". The "sisters" would originally have been members of a Christian church for a period of not less than seven years, with preference given to members of Christ Church, Westminster Bridge Road. The adjacent Vaughan almshouses were opened here in 1907, being removed from a site in Gravel Lane, Blackfriars Road, Southwark, and had a non-conformist benefactor, Mrs. Mary Sanction. Her Will provided for the maintenance of 24 poor women residing in the Parish of Christ Church, including a weekly allowance and the provision of a bottle of port wine on 25th April, the anniversary of the birth of Mrs. Elizabeth Vaughan, in whose memory the charity was founded. By permission of the Charity Commissioners, the administration of the two trusts was combined. The 1901 census demonstrates that the 20 inhabitants, all born in London, had an average age of 69.6 – this at a time when the life expectancy for women during the period 1891-1900 at age 65 was 11.3 years (10.3 years for men). Seen here are a group of residents dressed in their traditional garb, which included black shawls and bonnets, and possibly the resident custodian, Mr. Hibbins.

HILLS' BAKERY c. 1960

A master baker since 1926, Mr. Hills' business had started in 1949 at 36 Feltham Hill Road and also had a branch at Stainash Parade, Staines. In 1959 it was claimed that the firm were producing about a quarter of million articles of food a week and as well as supplying their regular clientele, Hills would also sell yeast to home bakers. Seen here outside their shop with the traditional design of handcart, their roundsman Mr. George Lock could offer selection of cakes and confectionery and regular orders of varieties of freshly baked bread. He had been working for local bakers since 1906, having started work at the age of 14, and retired in 1957. Hills' predecessors on the site, Bayley's bakery, advertised that it was founded in 1842, although it is not clear if this refers to the origins of Bennett's, whose premises they took over on lease in 1910, or their own origins. The growth of the trade in the area, like so many others, was fuelled by the rapid growth in the population and meant that by 1933 at least six retail bakers served area's population of c. 9,000: all of them offered a delivery service.

CONVENT ROAD AND ECCLESFIELD FIRE, 1907

Although it is not certain if the scene depicted here was photographed following a fire on 15th October, 1907, or on 7th April, 1921, the Good Shepherd Home occupying the Ecclesfield estate was the loser. The Good Shepherd Sisters had acquired the property in 1899 for £12,500 to establish an asylum under the Inebriates Act of 1899. In October 1899 there were 50 female inmates, mainly from Wormwood Scrubs and Holloway Prisons. By 1904 the Catholic Sisters had set up two separate homes, one voluntary and one fee-paying. The work of Ecclesfield was also financed by the on-site laundry and needlework which became well-established in the area. The fire of 1921 was a serious blow to the Order and resulted in the complete destruction of the chapel and all its fittings. An appeal for funds stated that there were 170 inmates in care here. It had been rebuilt by May 1922, but in 1933 proposed road improvements forced the sisters to seek alternative accommodation and they moved to Iden Manor, Staplehurst, Kent, in 1935.